# Explaining Long-Term Trends in Health and Longevity

*Explaining Long-Term Trends in Health and Longevity* is a collection of essays by Nobel laureate Robert W. Fogel on the theory and measurement of aging and health-related variables. Dr. Fogel analyzes historic data on height, health, nutrition, and life expectation to provide a clearer understanding of the past, illustrate the costs and benefits of using such measures, and note the difficulties of drawing conclusions from data intended for different purposes. Dr. Fogel explains how the basic findings of the anthropometric approach to historical analysis have helped reinterpret the nature of economic growth. Rising life expectancies and lower disease rates in countries experiencing economic growth highlight the importance of improving nutrition and agricultural productivity.

Robert W. Fogel is Charles R. Walgreen Distinguished Service Professor of American Institutions at the Booth School of Business, University of Chicago, and a research associate at the National Bureau of Economic Research. Dr. Fogel was the joint winner (with Douglass North) of the Nobel Prize in Economic Sciences in 1993. He is the author of several books, including *The Escape from Hunger and Premature Death, 1700–2100: Europe, America, and the Third World* (Cambridge University Press, 2004), and *The Fourth Great Awakening and the Future of Egalitarianism* (2002). He coauthored *The Changing Body: Health, Nutrition, and Human Development in the Western World since 1700* (Cambridge University Press, 2011).

# Explaining Long-Term Trends in Health and Longevity

ROBERT W. FOGEL

*University of Chicago*

CAMBRIDGE
UNIVERSITY PRESS

CAMBRIDGE UNIVERSITY PRESS
Cambridge, New York, Melbourne, Madrid, Cape Town,
Singapore, São Paulo, Delhi, Mexico City

Cambridge University Press
32 Avenue of the Americas, New York, NY 10013-2473, USA

www.cambridge.org
Information on this title: www.cambridge.org/9781107665811

First published 2012

Printed in the United States of America

*A catalog record for this publication is available from the British Library.*

*Library of Congress Cataloging in Publication Data*
Fogel, Robert William.
[Essays. Selections]
Explaining long-term trends in health and longevity / Robert W. Fogel.
pages   cm
Includes bibliographical references and index.
ISBN 978-1-107-02791-6 (hardback) – ISBN 978-1-107-66581-1 (paperback)
1. Medical economics – Longitudinal studies.   I. Title.
RA410.F64   2012
338.4′73621–dc23        2012011688

ISBN 978-1-107-02791-6 Hardback
ISBN 978-1-107-66581-1 Paperback

*To Steven Dennis Fogel and Michael Paul Fogel*

# Contents

# Tables

# Figures

# Acknowledgments

The chapters contained in this volume have benefited from the comments of a great many individuals, including George Alter, Jere Behrman, Roderick Floud, Patrick Galloway, John Komlos, Ronald D. Lee, S. R. Osmani, James Riley, J. M. Tanner, Amartya Sen, and E. A. Wrigley.

The author is grateful for the generosity of several individuals and institutions that have allowed previously published work to appear here. These include the editors of the *Journal of Interdisciplinary History* (MIT Press), which published a version of Chapter 2, and *Perspectives in Biology and Medicine* (Johns Hopkins University Press), which published versions of Chapters 4 and 5. A version of Chapter 3 was previously published in *Nutrition and Poverty* (Oxford University Press), edited by S. R. Osmani. Harry Kreisler, of the Institute of International Studies at the University of California, Berkeley, conducted the interview that comprises Chapter 7. The author thanks Stanley L. Engerman for his contribution of the foreword and for the suggestion of Cambridge University Press as a publisher for this work. Stanley L. Engerman, Roderick Floud, Gerald Friedman, Robert A. Margo, Kenneth Sokoloff, Richard H. Steckel, T. James Trussell, Georgia Villaflor, and Kenneth E. Wachter are coauthors of the original version of Chapter 2 and generously granted permission for its reproduction. Nathaniel Grotte prepared the manuscript and coordinated its publication with Cambridge University Press.

Much of the research discussed in this book draws from the research project *Early Indicators of Later Work Levels, Disease, and Death* (NIH Program Project grant P01 AG10120). The success of this project is the result of the contributions of a great many people over many years. The author gratefully acknowledges these contributions.

# 1

# Foreword

One of the most useful additions to the tools for the examination of long-term historical change has been the increased use of anthropometric data. These include information on height, health, nutrition, and life expectation. The use of these measures has been important for a wide range of historical questions, largely, but not limited to, those in economic history and including demography, development economics, and medical and nutritional history. Several decades back, when the historical uses of height were first introduced, such measures were only infrequently used. Indeed, such measures were often treated with skepticism or even, at times, with derision. As with most innovations, the acceptance of this approach required detailed empirical analysis and theoretical tests before acceptance was widespread. The major accomplishments of anthropometric history have established it as a central tool of comparative studies, over space as well as time. Among the major contributors to this body of research has been Robert Fogel, whose seminal work in this area covers a period of over two decades. This volume includes some of Fogel's published and unpublished works, indicating the breadth and depth of his studies as well as suggesting directions for further research.

The diverse sources of anthropometric information include data on heights, most frequently drawn from military recruitment records, which exist for numerous countries after the eighteenth century; data on mortality, drawn from statistics of death by age; and data on food supplies, based on records of agricultural production from censuses and other sources. However, some sources are unique to a particular time and place such as the mortality and health records resulting from the U.S. Civil War. This wide range of data permits the analysis of a broad spectrum of questions that can be of interest, particularly since they permit a very broad range of comparisons over time and geographical areas. Fogel's papers in this volume, some jointly authored but most singly authored, are an excellent example of the role anthropometric history has played in dealing with some new but also some traditional, historical problems.

These essays not only provide for a substantive understanding of the past but also illustrate the costs and benefits of using the measures, the difficulties of drawing interpretations from data prepared for quite different purposes, and the techniques that can be used to overcome the possible biases in the raw data. This broad sweep of concerns is seen particularly in Chapter 2, "Secular Changes in American and British Stature and Nutrition," which is the result of an early work in Fogel's broad project. The primary measure is of heights, used to measure changes in standards of living over time. On the basis of a variety of data sources for several different countries, including comparisons of American and British heights, and of American-born, Trinidadian-born, and African-born slaves, this analysis points to a number of interesting conclusions. These include the early achievement of modern levels of stature in the United States during and after the colonial period, the greater height of American adult males than those of England and elsewhere in Europe throughout the nineteenth century, and the greater height of U.S. slaves than those born in Trinidad and the even lower heights of those who were African born. These conclusions have proven robust in further studies, including one of the more unexpected of the results, that movements in heights did not always follow a linear trend but rather experienced cyclical fluctuations over time.

Chapter 3, "Second Thoughts on the European Escape from Hunger," studies British and French food consumption, heights, and mortality to provide several important historical points. The study of the time pattern of mortality, based primarily on the Wrigley–Schofield estimates, shows that the decline in British mortality was due mainly to improvements in overall consumption and real wages, with only a relatively small part due to the dramatic effects of declines in famine and harvest failures. Studies based on food availability suggest that in earlier centuries, a relatively large part of the population was not provided with adequate nutrition to be highly productive. In addition to indicating one key reason for limited economic growth in this period, the need for and provision of government-provided poor relief are highlighted.

Chapter 4, "Trends in Physiological Capital," follows one of the themes of the previous chapter, using data on the improvements in European heights in the nineteenth century to argue for a change from chronic malnutrition and reduced labor input to the expansion of work inputs related to better nutrition for the bulk of the population. The term *physiological capital* is a supplement to the more familiar terms of *human capital* and *health capital* and is used to explain not only the impact of higher birth weights on infant mortality but also the delayed onset of some chronic diseases and the increase in longevity. These developments are often ignored in explanations of economic growth, but as Fogel clearly demonstrates, they have played a major role in the process.

Chapter 5 uses several data sources to examine the role of childhood diseases in the subsequent development of chronic diseases. Consistent with previous arguments, Fogel points out that there has been a significant decline in disease rates, with the onset of these declining rates particularly marked after 1700 and accelerating in the course of the twentieth century. Noteworthy also was the decline in the inequality of heights and mortality within and between nations in this period, an indication of the broad diffusion of the benefits of increased agricultural productivity and therefore nutrition. These findings provide an important supplement to discussions of changing standards of living based exclusively on wage and income data.

The basic findings of the anthropometric approach to historical analysis have, as Fogel describes in the interview concluding the volume, meant some important reinterpretations of the nature of economic growth. The human body and its capacity at laboring and surviving have changed dramatically in those nations experiencing economic growth, highlighting the importance of agricultural productivity and improved nutrition. Clearly the physical capabilities of those in the developed nations in the twentieth century are quite different from those of their populations in the eighteenth and nineteenth centuries as well as from those in the less developed world today. Thus, as Fogel suggests, and his contributions demonstrate, new approaches and methods can lead to important new insights into historical changes.

– Stanley L. Engerman

# 2

# Secular Changes in American and British Stature and Nutrition

This chapter discusses the usefulness of data on height for the analysis of the impact of long-term changes in nutritional status and health on economic, social, and demographic behavior. In this chapter, measures of height are used for two related purposes. First, mean height at specific ages is used as a measure of the standard of living. When used in this way, data on height supplement other evidence such as indexes of real wages, estimates of per capita income, and measures of food consumption. One advantage of height data is their abundance and wide coverage of socioeconomic groups. Consequently, it is possible to develop continuous series for a wide range of geographical areas as well as for quite refined occupational categories. It is also possible to develop far more refined measures of the extent to which particular classes and areas were affected by changes in economic fortunes than has so far been possible through the use of either real wage indexes or measures of per capita income. Although it is unlikely that large bodies of height-by-age data will be uncovered for periods before 1700, the data are abundant from 1700 on, adding more than a century to most of the current series on per capita income. The wide geographical and occupational coverage offers the possibility that aggregate indexes constructed from them will be more representative of national trends

The coauthors of the original paper on which this chapter is based are Stanley L. Engerman, Roderick Floud, Gerald Friedman, Robert A. Margo, Kenneth Sokoloff, Richard H. Steckel, T. James Trussell, Georgia Villaflor, and Kenneth W. Wachter.

than are long-term wage indexes, which are composed of narrow, discontinuous series.[1]

## PRINCIPAL SAMPLES AND PROCEDURES

The chapter is based on a set of thirteen samples of data containing information on height-by-age and various socioeconomic variables that cover the period from 1750 through 1937 for the United States, Trinidad, Great Britain, and Sweden. Six of the samples are from U.S. military records for the period from 1750 to 1900. The other three U.S. samples contain information on both sexes: the sample of coastwise manifests provides information about slaves who boarded coastwise vessels between 1810 and 1863; the Fall River survey covers working children of school age during 1906–1907; and the cost of living survey covers all family members in a sample of households from 1934 to 1937. The Trinidad data set consists of complete censuses of the slaves on the island in 1813, with updates in 1814 and 1815, and then every three years until 1834.

One of the British samples is composed of poor boys from various parts of Great Britain, especially London, taken in by the Marine Society, a charitable organization, from 1750 to 1910; the other is

---

[1] Time series on height may be more reliable indicators of long-term changes in the welfare of the laboring classes than are the currently available indexes of real wages. Critics of the real wage indexes that have been computed for the eighteenth and nineteenth centuries, in both the United States and Great Britain, have noted the problems that beset the existing time series of nominal wages as well as the price deflators. The nominal wages for particular localities and particular occupations often remain relatively fixed over many years, sometimes even during periods of sharp fluctuations in the level of prices, so that the trend in real wages depends heavily on the choice of price indexes. Price deflators are generally lacking in information on the cost of shelter, which, in the more rapidly growing cities, may have accounted for more than one-quarter of the income of laborers. Efforts to turn wage indexes of particular occupations and localities into general regional or national wage indexes have produced nominal wage indexes, the movements of which are dominated for long periods of time by changes in a few occupations or localities and by discontinuities in underlying series. Von Tunzelmann's (1979) recent examination of the real wage series for England revealed that different reasonable ways of combining the individual series of nominal wage rates and the choice of different price deflators could imply either a rise of 250% in the national average of real wages between 1750 and 1850 or no rise at all. Data on height by occupation are more complete in their geographical scope than the wage data, especially for the lower-wage occupations, and do not need to be deflated by price indexes.

drawn from military recruitment records compiled between 1750 and 1910. The Swedish sample is drawn from muster rolls of army reserves who served from 1765 to 1885.

Measures of height are employed as the principal index of nutritional status. Both laboratory experiments on animal populations and observational studies of human populations have led physiologists and nutritionists to conclude that anthropometric measurements are reliable indexes of the extent of malnutrition among the socioeconomic classes of particular populations. Measures of height and weight at given ages, the age at which growth of stature terminates, attained final height, and especially the rate of change in height or weight during the growing ages "reflect accurately the state of a nation's public health and the average nutritional status of its citizens" (Eveleth and Tanner 1976, 1). Consequently, these measures are widely used by the World Health Organization and other agencies to assess the nutritional status of the populations of underdeveloped nations.[2]

The use of anthropometric measures as measures of nutrition rests on a well-defined pattern of human growth between childhood and maturity. The average annual increase in height (velocity) is greatest during infancy, falls sharply up to age three, and then falls more slowly throughout the remaining preadolescent years. During adolescence, velocity rises sharply to a peak that is approximately one-half of the velocity achieved during infancy, then falls sharply, and reaches zero at maturity. In girls, the adolescent growth spurt begins about two years earlier, and the magnitude of the spurt is slightly smaller than in boys. This growth pattern reflects the interaction of genetic, environmental, and socioeconomic factors during the period of growth. According to Eveleth and Tanner (1976, 176),

such interaction may be complex. Two genotypes which produce the same adult height under optimal environmental circumstances may produce different heights under circumstances of privation. Thus two children who would be the same height in a well-off community may not only both be smaller

---

[2] Appendix A of Fogel et al. (1982) summarizes the findings of the principal studies. For more extensive descriptions, see Tanner (1981, 1990). The relationship between height per capita income and the distribution of income in modern populations is analyzed in Steckel (1983). For a summary of the evidence on the relationship between anthropometric measures, nutrition, and health, see Eveleth and Tanner (1976) and Frisancho (1978).

under poor economic conditions, but one may be significantly smaller than the other. . . . If a particular environmental stimulus is lacking at a time when it is essential for the child (times known as "sensitive periods"), then the child's development may be shunted, as it were, from one line to another.

The relative importance of environmental and genetic factors in explaining individual variations in height is still a matter of some debate. For most well-fed contemporary populations, however, systematic genetic influences appear to have a modest impact on mean heights. For example, the mean heights of well-fed Western Europeans, North American whites, and North American blacks are similar. There are some ethnic groups in which mean final heights of well-fed persons today differ significantly from the Western European or North American standards; in these cases, the deviation from the European standard appears to be due to genetic factors. However, because such ethnic groups have represented a miniscule proportion of American and European populations, they are irrelevant to an explanation of the observed secular trends in mean final heights in the United States and in the various European nations since 1750, nor can they account for differences at various points of time between the means in the final heights of the U.S. population and the principal populations from which the population was drawn. In this connection, it should be noted that today, the mean final heights of well-fed males in the main African nations from which the U.S. black population is derived also fall within the narrow band designated as the Western European standard.[3]

Physiologists, anthropologists, and nutritionists have charted the effect of nutritional deficiencies on the human growth profile. Short periods of severe malnutrition or prolonged periods of moderate malnutrition merely delay the adolescent growth spurt; severe, prolonged

[3] The belief that heterosis (hybrid vigor) would make Americans substantially taller than the ethnic groups from which they were drawn has not been sustained by previous anthropometric research. See Cavalli-Sforza and Bodmer (1971) for a theoretical argument as to why the effect of heterosis in human populations is small. Our investigations have failed to yield consistent signs on dummy variables for either males or females born of mixed unions. The magnitudes of the positive coefficients for adults, not all of which are statistically significant, fall in the range of 0.17–0.66 inches. The average of all the coefficients so far estimated for adults ($N = 9$) is 0.19 inches. Even this small difference is not necessarily due to heterosis; it might reflect differences in treatment during the growing years (Eveleth and Tanner 1976; Fogel et al. 1982).

malnutrition may diminish the typical growth spurt pattern and contribute to substantial permanent stunting. If malnutrition is both prolonged and moderate, growth will continue beyond the age at which the growth of well-fed adolescents ceases. Hence the average age at which the growth spurt peaks, the average age at which growth terminates, the mean height during adolescent ages, and the mean final height are all important indicators of mean nutritional status. Any one of these factors can be used to trace secular trends in nutrition. The more of these measures that are available, the more precise is the determination of the severity and duration of periods of malnutrition.

In considering the relationship between nutrition and height, it is important to stress that height is a net rather than a gross measure of nutrition. Moreover, although changes in height during the growing years are sensitive to current levels of nutrition, mean final heights reflect the accumulated past nutritional experience stretching not only over the growing years of the individuals measured but over the lifetimes of their mothers and perhaps of their grandmothers as well. Thus, when mean final heights are used to explain differences in productivity, they reveal the effect not of current levels of nutrition on productivity but of the net nutritional levels during the growing years of the measured individuals and, to an extent still to be established, of conditions during their mothers' and grandmothers' lives.

The measure of net nutrition represented by mean heights depends on the intake of nutrients, on the amount of nutrients available for physical growth after the necessary claims of work and other activities (including recovery from infections), and on the efficiency with which the body converts nutrients into outputs. The body's ability to generate a surplus for growth will vary with such factors as age; the climate; the nature of the available food, clothing, and shelter; the disease environment; the intensity of work; and the quality of public sanitation. The same nutritional input can have varying effects, depending on environmental conditions. The differing nutritional requirements for different intensities of work and other environmental conditions suggest that changes in the level of gross input (measured by food consumption) might not provide a full indication of changes in the nutrients available for physical growth. It is important to stress that although mean height measures the cumulative effect of the nutrients available after allowing for physical maintenance, work, and the impact of the man-made and natural environment, it does not by itself indicate whether fluctuations in net nutrition are due to changes in the consumption of food, the claims on the food intake, or the efficiency with which food is converted into outputs.[4]

It cannot be assumed that there has been an invariable relationship, regardless of time and place, between height and such other important variables as occupation, wealth, literacy, ethnicity, residence, fertility, mortality, morbidity, migration, and a variety of intergenerational variables. Much attention has been devoted to determining which relationships are stable and which are not and to the determination of the factors that have been influential in shifting relationships.

Although the findings to date are illuminating, the process of mapping the relationship between height and various socioeconomic variables is still in progress. Each new finding raises new questions, and the answers frequently require a search for new data sets or the construction of new variables from the existing data sets. Many of the new issues point to the need to bring intergenerational variables to bear on the analysis. Some of the progress along these lines has been made in the study of the Trinidad data. Work has been initiated that links data on height in other samples with genealogies and with census data on the households in which the persons measured were raised. This work makes it possible to investigate the influence of the nutritional status of parents and grandparents on the health and productivity of their children and grandchildren.[5]

---

[4] It has sometimes been argued that it is impossible to separate, by statistical analyses, the effect on growth of disease and of a generally inadequate level of food intake. This argument assumes a much higher level of collinearity than actually exists. It is true that the body draws more heavily on nutritional stores when it is fighting an infection than when it is not, so that an infection may cause growth to cease during a period of infection. However, as Nevin S. Scrimshaw has pointed out, if a child is normally well fed, and if there is sufficient time between infectious episodes, there will usually be full catch-up when an infection ceases. Normal, well-fed children do not grow at equal daily rates but alternate periods of growth well in excess of the daily average, with periods of little or no growth as disease and other claims on nutritional intake wax and wane. In well-fed children, these lacunae in growth have no effect on final heights because of full and rapid catch-up, but in malnourished children, they contribute to permanent stunting.

[5] Cf. Chapter 4 and Chandra (1975), Tanner (1990), and Barker (1998). In the case of the Civil War data set, recruits have been linked with pension records that give pensioners' medical histories (including degrees of impairment of productivity at various

Because much of what is known about the socioeconomic determinants of height-by-age profiles is based on observations of modern populations, particularly in relatively rich nations, the usefulness of this knowledge for historical analysis is still under study. Because past conditions of malnourishment and health may have been far worse than those prevailing in many poor countries today, possible departures from currently known variations in the shape of the height-by-age profile are still under investigation. The work so far indicates that although exceedingly severe conditions led to variations in growth patterns, the general patterns established from the study of modern populations appear to apply to historical populations as far back as the beginning of the eighteenth century.

### STATISTICAL ISSUES

Use of military data raises questions about the extent to which soldiers and sailors were representative of the underlying populations from which these data were drawn. The problem is more severe in volunteer than in conscript armies. Volunteer armies, especially in peacetime, are selective in their admission criteria and often have minimum height requirements. Consequently, even if information on rejectees exists, the question of the extent to which applicants are self-screened remains. In many conscript armies, virtually all males of eligible age, including those who offer substitutes or are otherwise excused, are examined and measured.

Our procedures rest on a combination of theoretical considerations, empirical information, and simulation techniques. Much of the power of these techniques hinges on the fact that the distribution of final heights is well described by a normal distribution. The standard deviation of this distribution is rather tightly bounded for European, North American, and Afro-American populations. Regardless of the ethnicity or the socioeconomic conditions of the population in question, the standard deviations appear to fall in the range of 2.6 ± 0.6 inches.[6]

---

ages) between 1865 and their death. This linked sample is being used to analyze the effect of childhood malnutrition on adult morbidity, labor productivity, and health.

[6] This is the case in large samples of complete populations. For smaller samples, the range of the standard deviation is larger. For further evidence, see Kemsley (1951), Karpinos (1958), and U.S. National Center for Health Statistics (1965).

The distribution of height at each age during growing years is not normal but is nearly so.[7]

## SAMPLE-SELECTION BIASES

Use of military records to measure trends in height calls attention to a variety of sample-selection biases, the most important of these being the problem of left-tail truncation, which is characteristic of both the U.S. and British peacetime armies. Before turning to this issue, two others need to be considered: the self-selection bias of volunteers and whether persons rejected for reasons other than height are nevertheless shorter than those accepted.

There is clearly evidence of self-selection bias in volunteer armies. Persons of foreign birth and native-born laborers living in cities are overrepresented, whereas native-born individuals living in rural areas are underrepresented. Since there are significant differences in height among these groups, it is necessary to standardize for these characteristics in estimating the trend in aggregate heights. Necessary weights are available from federal censuses and other sources. Much of the interest turns on secular trends in the heights of particular groups that, even if underrepresented, are nevertheless present in sufficient numbers to permit analysis.

There is the issue of whether volunteers in particular subgroups (e.g., blue-collar urban laborers aged twenty to twenty-five) are representative of the class from which they are drawn. Our approach to this question is to compare the characteristics of the volunteers in the peacetime army with individuals of the same subgroups in wartime armies subject to conscription (World War II), or in armies in which a very high proportion of those of military age were examined (the Civil War), or in scientifically designed random samples (such as the national sample of 1960–1962). Most of our work to date has focused on the records of the Union Army. The Civil War involved a larger proportion of persons of military age than any other war in American history. Approximately 95 percent of white males between the ages of eighteen and twenty-five in the Union states were examined, and

---

[7] The standard deviation of height follows a pattern during the adolescent growth spurt that is quite similar to the velocity profile. It rises as the growth spurt approaches, reaches a peak at the peak of the growth spurt, and then declines to the level just before the onset of the spurt (cf. Trussell and Steckel 1978).

approximately 75 percent of the examinees were inducted. The results of our investigation so far indicate that with respect to height, volunteers from particular subgroups are representative of the subgroups from which they are drawn, although we are still at an early stage in this investigation. If subsequent research should indicate biases so far undetected, that work will also provide the desired correction factors.[8]

There remains the question of whether persons actually inducted into the army but rejected for reasons other than height were shorter than those accepted. The World War II data analyzed by Karpinos (1958) show that 41 percent of all those called for examination were rejected and that rejectees were an average of 0.22 inches shorter than those inducted. Consequently, the failure to take account of rejectees would bias the estimated mean final height of the overall population upward by 0.09 inches. Although a bias of this magnitude is statistically significant because of the large sample size, it is too small to have a significant effect on most of the points at issue in this study. The data presented by Baxter indicate that the bias arising from persons rejected because of disease in the Union Army introduces an upward bias of 0.03 inches in the estimated final height of the overall population.[9]

### MEASUREMENT BIAS

These are a series of issues regarding the reliability of measures pertaining to the height-by-age schedule. Some relate to the accuracy of the age information and some to the accuracy of the height information. Issues regarding age include whether ages were heaped, were reported to the nearest or the last birthday, or were arbitrarily assigned on the basis of height. Issues regarding height include whether there was heaping on even heights, whether heights were rounded to the nearest inch (or fraction of an inch) rather than to the last full inch (or fraction thereof), and whether individuals were measured with or without shoes.

---

[8] U.S. National Center for Health Statistics (1965). These figures are estimated from data in Gould (1869), hereinafter referred to as the Gould Report; Baxter (1875), hereinafter referred to as the Baxter Report; and U.S. Provost-Marshal-General (1866).

[9] Karpinos (1958). The bias in height is computed from the Baxter Report, II, table 16, by fitting normal curves to the data on the distribution of the heights of rejectees and recruits.

Accuracy in age has little bearing on the determination of the secular trend in final heights because it is of little importance whether a person classified as thirty is actually twenty-eight or thirty-two. Such heaping is of some importance during the growing years. There is evidence of age heaping at ages ten and twenty and at the minimum age for recruitment into military organizations. Although such heaping will add perturbation to the height-velocity profile, it does not usually affect the determination of the age at which the profile peaks. A more serious issue arises in the case of the coastwise manifests, where it has been suggested that ages were arbitrarily assigned on the basis of height. If that were true, however, the standard deviation of height would not, as it does, have the characteristic pattern of increasing and then decreasing as the peak of the growth spurt is approached and surpassed.[10]

Heaping on even inches is evident even when the measurement is conducted by qualified personnel (as in the national sample of 1960–1962). In military organizations with minimum height requirements, there is further evidence of heaping at the inch just above the cutoff. Simulation models indicate that even-number heaping does not introduce a systematic bias. Although it may affect the accuracy of estimates of mean height, even with large amounts of heaping (in the range of 15%–30%), the error will be in the neighborhood of one-tenth of an inch. With respect to rounding, from the earliest date for which military records are available, the standard practice was to round to the nearest inch or fraction of an inch. A study of actual practice in World War II revealed a slight tendency to round downward, which introduced an average error of 0.2 inches. There is no reason to assume that this tendency has changed over time. Our analysis of the data in the Union Army records indicates that the bias may be due mainly to a tendency to round the heights of tall persons who should have been measured at fractional inches downward to the nearest inch. In any case, the magnitude of this error will not seriously distort secular trends, nor should it significantly affect the cross-sectional analysis of the relationship between height and economic or demographic factors.[11]

---

[10] Trussell and Steckel (1978).

[11] Karpinos (1958); U.S. National Center for Health Statistics (1965).

In the case of the coastwise manifests and the colonial muster rolls, the question arises as to whether individuals were measured with or without shoes. To resolve this question, we have turned to data on people recruited into the Union Army or the regular army, where individuals are known to have been measured without shoes. The Gould report contains a sample of black recruits born in the slave states who were aged twenty-five and older ($N = 13,653$). The mean height in this sample, 67.2 inches, is virtually identical with the mean height (67.1 inches) computed for the same category in the coastwise manifests. Similarly, those recruited into the regular U.S. Army who were born between 1771 and 1790 averaged 68.3 inches ($N = 611$), which exceeds the mean height in the Revolutionary sample by 0.2 inches.[12]

## METHODS OF ESTIMATING MEAN HEIGHT FROM TRUNCATED DISTRIBUTIONS

For many of our files, the possibility of obtaining useful information from the height-by-age data depends on solving the problem of selection bias due to truncation or shortfall in the height distribution, particularly for lower heights. Various distortions of the true underlying distribution of heights in the population contributing soldiers and sailors are to be expected in military height distributions, including heaping on whole or even numbers of inches, oversampling in the center of the distribution, and occasional undersampling of high heights. Although some distortions are apparent in all our bodies of data, the problem of undersampling of small heights is particularly acute for the regular armed forces of Britain and the United States. These organizations set minimum height limits at different times, varying with military needs, sometimes shifting frequently and sometimes ranging as high as 67 inches. Minimum height standards were flexibly enforced so that very sharp cutoffs are not usually apparent in the data. It appears that

---

[12] Gould Report, 147. The Baxter sample was limited to military units where men were measured without shoes. Baxter (I, 14–15) conjectured that the recruits in some of the units in the Gould sample were measured with shoes. However, for the ages shown in Table 2.1, the Baxter and Gould samples yield mean heights that differ from each other by less than one-tenth of an inch. This finding indicates that the proportion of the men in the Union Army who may have been measured with shoes was too small to affect the analysis.

in some cases, 30 or 40 percent of the small heights in the underlying distribution may be missing. Such undersampling could vitiate the information content of the data, unless reliable statistical procedures are employed to correct for the problem.

An important aspect of our project has been the development of statistical estimators that perform reliably in the presence of undersampling of small heights. These estimators must also cope with the other distortions that we suspect in the observed distributions. The multiple distortions make our problem more complicated than most undersampling problems treated in the statistical literature, even though some ideas presented in the literature may be capable of extension.[13]

Our problem occurs at two levels. The first is the estimation of average height of an underlying distribution for men old enough to attain their terminal heights. A normal distribution for terminal heights is both well established for contemporary data and consistent with the examination of our files, and the assumption of normality for the underlying distribution places our problem into a well-defined parametric framework. We are also faced with the problem of how to estimate the mean of a distribution of height at a given age during the ages of growth. Modern data indicate that the underlying distributions during adolescence are at first skewed to the right, as early maturers attain peak growth velocity, and then skewed to the left, when only late maturers still await their growth spurt.

Our two principal methods for correcting left-tail censoring, the quantile bend method (QQ) and the maximum likelihood method (RSMLE), are described in two papers. Extension of the RSMLE method to regression analysis is reported in a third paper. These methods have been tested extensively both by Monte Carlo techniques and by simulation techniques on actual distributions of heights; the tests have shown both to be generally reliable.[14]

One of the tests, for example, was performed on a sample of the heights of London schoolchildren for 1965. The data consist of complete (i.e., nontruncated) distributions at each age during the growth spurt. Sample sizes varied from 801 to 2,493; the absolute value of

[13] See, e.g., Cohen (1950), Harter and Moore (1966), and Poirier (1978).
[14] Wachter (1981), Wachter and Trussell (1982), and Trussell and Wachter (1984), respectively.

the coefficient of skewness ($\gamma_1$) varied from 0.031 to −0.201. Our procedure was to use our estimators to infer the true mean of the distribution under conditions of increasing truncation. The truncation was allowed to range from 0 to 80 percent of the distribution (truncating from the lower end). The particular point at issue was whether techniques devised to cope with truncation of normal distributions would be reliable when applied to an estimation of distributions of height at growing ages, which are positively skewed during the rising portion of the growth spurt and negatively skewed during the declining portion. This effect was first discovered by Boas in 1892 and was documented by Tanner using London County Council data for 1955. The degree of skewing is statistically significant but small enough so that the distribution is treated as normal in the estimation of the centiles that demarcate the bounds for normal adolescent development. Nevertheless, it was necessary to determine whether even such moderate skewing would mislead our estimators in situations in which such skewing is combined with truncation.[15]

The estimators achieved nearly perfect results before truncation, demonstrating that skewing was too small to require the abandonment of the normal approximation in this case.[16] The estimators generally continued to behave well even with truncation of up to 50 percent of the original distribution. The RSMLE estimator performed very well with both continuous and grouped data. At levels of truncation below 50 percent, it consistently produced estimates close to the true mean, although there was a tendency to overcorrect, that is, to produce estimates slightly below the true mean. The accuracy of the RSMLE estimator decreased with truncation above the modal value. The QQ estimator was generally correct, even with truncation above 50 percent.

THE "BASKETBALL" PROBLEM

It has been argued that one cannot assume, merely from the fact that a military distribution appears to be closely approximated by a normal or a truncated normal distribution, that the mean of the distribution may be taken as a reasonable estimate of the mean final height of

[15] Tanner (1959).
[16] A conclusion previously reached in Tanner et al. (1965).

males in civilian life. The issue raised here goes beyond biases of the type already considered. Persons rejected for reasons other than height, as we have seen, are only slightly shorter than those accepted (less than one-tenth of an inch in the Civil War case), and the self-selection biases served to favor particular socioeconomic subgroups rather than to distort the height distribution of these subgroups.

What is at issue in the "basketball" problem is the possibility that the sampling criteria of the military organizations might produce distributions of height that, although normal, have a much higher mean height than that of the general population of adult males. In this connection, it is argued that one cannot use the normality of a given distribution as evidence of its representativeness. It is further suggested that if procedures such as those that we have developed were applied to the height distribution of players in the National Basketball Association (NBA), we would discover that this distribution was also normal so that careless application of our procedures could lead to the erroneous conclusion that the mean height of American males was 78 inches.

Clearly one cannot use the mere normality of a military distribution as evidence that it represents the overall adult civilian distribution – among other reasons because the height distribution of each of the major socioeconomic subgroups in the population is also normal, although their means are significantly different. The power of the QQ procedure lies in what it tells us about height distributions that depart from normality. The distortions in such distributions are clues that, when carefully analyzed, suggest the nature of the selection or self-selection criteria that produced the distortions.[17]

The usefulness of our procedures is well illustrated by applying them to the distribution of heights in the NBA. Figure 2.1 shows the QQ plot for the NBA. If the distribution of heights were normal, the plot should form a straight line, with the mean of the distribution given by the intersection of the plot with the zero ordinate. As can be seen in Figure 2.1A, the plot of the NBA distribution is irregular, unlike

---

[17] Theoretically, if the heights of each of the subgroups of a population are normally distributed but have different means, the overall population cannot be normally distributed and have the same standard deviation as the subpopulations. Nevertheless, the normal distribution gives a good fit to the overall distribution in such data sets as the Union Army as well as to each of the major subgroups, and the standard deviations are generally quite similar.

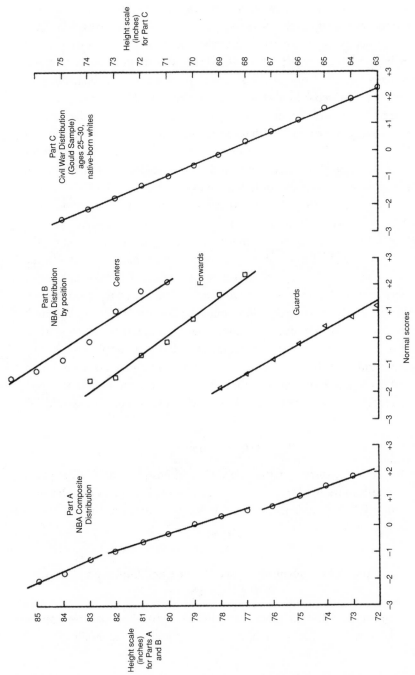

FIGURE 2.1. Application of the QQ procedure to the basketball problem.

19

the Civil War distribution of heights in Figure 2.1C. On inspection, it appears that the NBA distribution might actually consist of at least two, and possibly three, straight-line segments. In other words, the plot in Figure 2.1A suggests that the NBA distribution of heights might actually be the result of a composite of three normal distributions. Indeed, when separate distributions are computed for guards, centers, and forwards, we obtain three single-peaked distributions that appear to be censored normals, with means at 74.4, 80.2, and 83.4 inches (see Figure 2.1B). Thus it appears that the managers of teams in the NBA have target heights for each position. Target heights may yield normal distributions even if the underlying population from which the sample is being drawn is highly skewed (as is the extreme right-hand tail of the distribution of adult heights).[18]

It follows that when working with military data, one should take into account the sampling strategy of particular military units. In the case of the U.S. Army, official orders that established the standard for recruiting in different units have been published. In the British case, the standards are described in unpublished orders. The most common procedure was to have a minimum height requirement, which shifted, up or down, depending on the demand for and supply of recruits. Some units, such as the cavalry and the navy, had both minimum and maximum requirements. Only a few parade companies had target heights, which were their ideal but which they did not always achieve.

### THE FINDINGS

The secular pattern of native-born U.S. whites prior to 1910 appears to be substantially different from that of most European populations. Similarly, the experience of U.S. blacks diverged from that of blacks born in the Caribbean or in Africa.

### The Early Achievement of Modern Stature and Improved Nutrition in the United States

By the time of the American Revolution, native-born whites appear to have achieved nearly modern final heights. The analysis of a

---

[18] Hollander (1979); the plot in Figure 2.1C is based on data in the Gould report, 96, 101.

TABLE 2.1. *Mean Final Heights of U.S. Native-Born White Males in Three Wars*

|  | Age Category (years) | Sample Size | Sample Mean (inches) | Standard Error (inches) |
|---|---|---|---|---|
| American Revolution | 24–35 | 968 | 68.1 | 0.08 |
| Civil War |  |  |  |  |
| Gould sample | 25–30 | 123,472 | 68.2 | 0.01 |
| Baxter sample | 25–34 | 54,931 | 68.2 |  |
| World War II | 20–24 | 119,443 | 68.2 | 0.01 |

*Note:* Computed from data in colonial muster rolls, the Gould report, the Baxter report, and Karpinos, "Height and Weight." The Revolutionary, Gould, and Baxter samples are based on inductees. The World War II sample falls in the twenty to twenty-four age category. The data in Baxter's summary do not permit the calculation of the standard error of the mean. Data presented by Karpinos indicate that inductees were about 0.09 inches taller than examinees. Data presented by Baxter indicate that inductees were 0.03 inches taller than examinees. Only the Revolutionary sample has been corrected for truncation bias. Preliminary analyses indicate that such corrections would not reduce the figures shown for the Civil War and World War II samples by more than 0.2 inches.

sample of recruits from the Revolutionary Army (1775–1783) indicates that the final height of native-born white males between the ages of twenty-four and thirty-five averaged 68.1 inches. This figure is not only 1–4 inches greater than the final height of European males reported for several nations during the late seventeenth and early eighteenth centuries but is also virtually identical with final heights in the Union Army during the Civil War and in the U.S. Army during World War II (see Table 2.1). Extending the analysis to a sample of recruits during the French and Indian War (1756–1763) indicates that final heights were increasing during the middle of the eighteenth century. After controlling for place of birth, place of residence, and occupation, cohorts born between 1740 and 1765 were 0.4 inches taller ($t = 2.4$) than those born between 1715 and 1739. Because cohorts born before 1740 still attained final heights that averaged above 67.5 inches, it appears likely that improvements in nutrition began early and were quite rapid in America.[19]

[19] The evidence on adult heights in Europe during the eighteenth and early nineteenth centuries has not generally been analyzed for secular trends and in some cases has not yet been adequately analyzed for truncation bias. The principal studies of European heights during this period are cited in Fogel et al. (1982, appendix A). Only the series for Norway (Kiil 1939) and the sample of Swedish heights retrieved and analyzed by

This inference is supported by data on food consumption in Massachusetts discovered by McMahon. Wills deposited in Middlesex County between 1654 and 1830 indicate a sharp rise in the average amount of meat annually allotted to widows for their consumption. Between circa 1675 and circa 1750, the average allotment increased from approximately 80 to approximately 165 pounds per annum. Over the next seventy-five years, allotments rose more gradually, reaching 200 pounds at the end of the first quarter of the nineteenth century. The evidence both on stature and on food allotments suggests that Americans achieved an average level of meat consumption by the middle of the eighteenth century that was not achieved in Europe until well into the twentieth century.[20]

### Cycles in Height

The estimated mean final heights of males for the three wars reported in Table 2.1 do not necessarily imply a perfectly flat secular trend between circa 1778 and circa 1943. Contrary to the popular impression that there have been continuous increases in height and secular improvements in nutrition, the evidence analyzed in this project indicates that there may actually have been cycles in height of both native-born whites and blacks residing (but not necessarily born) in the United States.

Analysis of information contained in the coastwise manifests indicates that the final heights of slaves born in the early 1790s were approximately 0.5 inches less than those of slaves born in the late 1770s (see Figure 2.2). The final heights of cohorts born after 1790 increased for approximately twenty years so that cohorts born after 1815 were slightly taller than cohorts born during the late 1770s and 1780s. Thereafter, final heights remained fairly steady at approximately 67.3 inches for cohorts born through the early 1830s. The data in the manifests now available are too sparse to carry the analysis of this time trend beyond cohorts born in the early 1830s. But the data on blacks taken from the Union Army muster rolls, which mesh quite well with the results from slave manifests for overlapping cohorts, indicate that

Sandberg and Steckel (1987) provide continuous series that reach back to the first half of the eighteenth century.

[20] Holmes (1907); McMahon (1980).

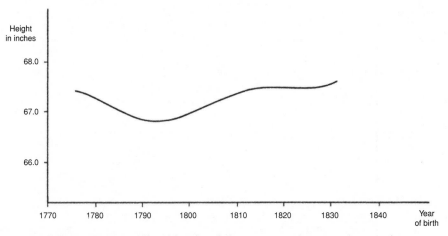

FIGURE 2.2. Time profile of height of slave men aged twenty-three to forty-nine. *Source:* Slave manifests ($n = 9,726$).

cohorts born in the late 1830s and early 1840s may have experienced a decline in final heights that was even sharper than that experienced by cohorts born between 1780 and 1795.[21]

The time trend in the final height of northern, native-born whites is somewhat different from that of U.S. slaves. The rising trend observed for cohorts born before the Revolution levels off and appears to have remained fairly steady for cohorts born between the Revolution and the end of the 1790s. The regular army data needed to continue the trend from 1800 to 1819 have not yet been processed, but the preliminary analysis of a subsample ($N = 773$) of Union Army records bearing on this period, which covers only the last few years of the teens, suggests that cohorts born during the first two decades may have experienced increasing final heights. It also appears that their upward trend leveled during the 1820s and then declined (see Figure 2.3). Over a period of fifteen years, the decline in the final heights of native-born whites appears to have been about 1 inch.

---

[21] Analyses of trends in heights of adolescent slaves confirm the general pattern revealed by adult heights, except that the amplitudes of the cycles in adolescent heights are even greater than they are in final heights (Steckel 1983). Taken together, the evidence on adolescents and adults suggests that there were periods of deterioration in the nutritional status and health of slaves that substantially retarded their rate of development during adolescence but that this loss in tempo was partly compensated by a longer period of growth that permitted some "catching up."

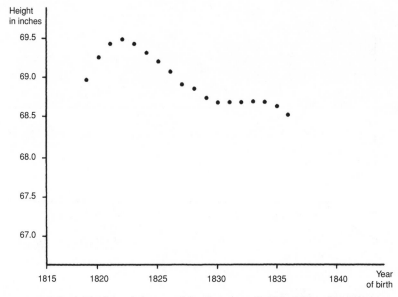

FIGURE 2.3. An index of the trend in the mean final heights of U.S. native-born whites, by birth cohort, 1819–1836. *Source:* Preliminary sample of Union Army muster rolls ($N = 533$). Estimated from data on recruits into the Union Army who were between ages twenty-five and forty-four at the time of measurement.

There is evidence of a cycle in stature between the Civil War and World War II. Table 2.2 shows that final height increased at a rate of 1.2 inches per generation between the cohorts born circa 1906 and circa 1921; between the circa 1921 and circa 1931 cohorts, the rate was 2.7 inches per generation. Obviously, even the 1.2-inch rate could not have extended back to the Civil War. That would require the final height of circa 1863 to have been approximately 2 inches below the level indicated by the Gould and Baxter samples. Indeed, since the final height of the circa 1906 cohort is about 0.5 inches below the final height shown in the Civil War data, at some time between circa 1863 and circa 1926 (1906 + 20), final height declined.

Preliminary analysis of the British data has been focused on the trend in heights in London of adolescent boys from poor families over the period from 1770 to 1870. This analysis reveals that the mean height of boys between the ages of fourteen and sixteen from families of laboring classes was relatively steady from circa 1775 to circa

TABLE 2.2. *Twentieth-Century Growth Rates in Mean Final Height of U.S. Males (Estimated from Cohorts Measured c. 1943 and c. 1961)*

*Part A: Mean Final Heights Arranged by Cohorts*

| Age Category When Measured (years) | Sample Size | Midpoint of the Interval in Which Cohort Was Born | Mean Height at Time of Measurement |
|---|---|---|---|
| From U.S.D.H.E.W. (1965) | | | |
| 1. 25–34 | 10,281 | 1931 | 69.11 |
| 2. 35–44 | 11,373 | 1921 | 68.22 |
| From Karpinos | | | |
| 3. 20–24 | 141,803 | 1921 | 68.15 |
| 4. 25–29 | 99,786 | 1916 | 68.06 |
| 5. 30–34 | 96,704 | 1911 | 67.81 |
| 6. 35–37 | 53,624 | 1906.5 | 67.58 |

*Part B: Growth Rates per Generation between Cohorts*

| Interval over Which Growth Rate Is Calculated, by Birth of Cohort | Growth Rates (in inches per 30 years) |
|---|---|
| 1921–1931 | 2.7 |
| 1906.5–1921 | 1.2 |

*Note:* Data from longitudinal studies of stature indicate that shrinkage does not usually begin before age 50 (Tanner, private communication). If taller individuals were more likely to survive to a given age, the estimated growth rates would be biased downward, but the size of the bias would be small. If, for example, those who died between ages thirty and forty were 1 inch shorter on average than those who survived to age forty, then (using the applicable life table in Preston et al. 1972) one would have to reduce the height of the c. 1921 cohort by 0.03 inches before computing the 1921–1931 growth rate. This change would increase the 1921–1931 growth rate from 2.70 to 2.77 per generation (Karpinos 1958; U.S. National Center for Health Statistics 1965).

1790 and then declined for two decades, the lowest point coming somewhere near 1810. The extent of the decline was about 1.5 inches. From circa 1810 to circa 1838, mean heights increased rapidly, at a rate of 2 inches per decade, so that the maximum previous mean was exceeded by 1820. After circa 1838, heights again appear to have declined, but the new rate of decline was only about 0.2 inches over a period of twenty years, after standardizing for socioeconomic characteristics.

The exact timing of the sharp rise in height following the close of the Napoleonic wars is still under investigation. Although future work on statistical issues might lead to an expansion or compression of the period of rapid increases in heights, it is clear that poor adolescent boys in London were about 4 inches taller after 1838 than their counterparts had been before 1790. Indeed, the adolescent poor of London in the late eighteenth century were so short that only two of the eighty-one ethnic groups for which modern height data are available record lower adolescent heights. These are the Lumi and Bundi of New Guinea – two exceedingly impoverished populations. Even after the period of rapid increase, poor London boys were still short by modern British standards; at age fourteen, they were about 5 inches shorter than British boys of the same age today – a gap that is due partly to the slow rate of physical maturation and partly to malnutrition, probably early in life, that shifted the whole growth profile downward.

### The Influence of Economic and Social Factors on Height

Multivariate regression analysis has been applied to several of the samples under study to relate final heights to such economic characteristics as occupation, migration experience, urban birth or residence, race, and place of birth. At the present time, with a few exceptions, the analyses have been limited to the information about each individual contained in the records on height. However, work is now under way to link information on the individuals and their families in the manuscript schedules of censuses, in probate and tax lists, and in other records. For example, the individuals included in the sample from the muster rolls of the Union Army are now being linked with information on their households contained in the manuscript schedules of the 1850, 1860, and 1870 censuses and with the pension records on these individuals and their heirs, usually filed late in their life or shortly after their death. In this way, it is possible to obtain relevant information on the individuals, not only at the age of enlistment but also during their growing years and in their later lives. Such linking also allows an analysis of the effect of intergenerational factors (such as the ethnicity, wealth, and social status of parents and grandparents) on the development of children and grandchildren. Where such interrelationships cannot be established through direct linking at the household level, it is possible to use cross-sectional regression techniques, with counties or similar geographical divisions as the unit of observation, to analyze the nexus between height and relevant social and economic variables.

The regressions so far performed on the muster rolls of the French and Indian War, the Revolutionary War, the regular army during the early national period, and the Civil War show that in all four periods (1756–1763, 1775–1783, 1815–1820, and 1861–1865), persons of foreign birth were about an inch or more shorter than those of native birth. There was a significant shift over time in the impact of urban–rural residence on the final heights of the native born. Beginning with final heights virtually identical with native-born persons of urban birth, native-born persons of rural birth gained an advantage of 0.5 inches by the second decade of the nineteenth century, and this gap continued, if not widened, down to the time of the Civil War. There were also significant shifts over time in the relationship between occupation and stature. From only minor discrepancies in final heights between farmers and other occupational groups during the colonial period, significant differences had emerged by the time of the Civil War. Blue-collar recruits were nearly 0.8 inches shorter than farmers, after adjusting for urban–rural and nativity status. In all four time periods, the cross-sectional regressions yielded statistically significant coefficients on region of birth, race, and migratory experience.

Because ex-slaves in the Union Army were geographically concentrated, the sample already in hand is large enough to experiment with cross-sectional analysis at the county level. The analysis of final heights was performed on a sample of 913 ex-slaves who were between the ages of twelve and seventeen at the time of the 1850 census. On average, ex-slaves were about 1 inch shorter than were native-born whites. Moreover, slaves from the Deep South states, which specialized in cotton and rice, were shorter than those from border states engaged in tobacco and general farming. These state differentials appear to be explained by the positive correlation of height with per capita corn production, a negative correlation with the median size of the slave plantation, and a negative correlation with urbanization.[22]

In the case of the London boys, there is abundant information on their socioeconomic characteristics before they entered the Marine Society, which may be relevant in explaining variations in heights. However, an analysis of this information is retarded by the limited

---

[22] Because corn was mainly a feed crop, corn per capita may be viewed as a proxy for meat per capita.

range of differences in the occupational categories, by variations in the minimum height standard, and by the rapid pace of change. Two characteristics that do appear as significant determinants of height so far are addresses outside London (associated with taller boys) and the designation "destitute" (with shortness).[23]

### The Influence of Height on Social and Economic Behavior

One of the bodies of data recently analyzed bears on the impact of height on the productivity of manual laborers. Some commanders of the Union Army treated runaway slaves as contraband of war, and so, in addition to recording some of the usual information found in muster rolls, they also included information on the value of the slaves. One such contraband list, discovered in records for Mississippi, has recently been analyzed. The mean height of the 523 adult males in this sample was 67.4 inches, with a standard deviation of 2.8 inches – almost identical to the corresponding figures for Mississippi recruits obtained in the main sample of black companies.[24]

Regression analysis revealed that the value of slaves was positively associated with both height and weight. A slave of average weight for his height who was one standard deviation taller than the mean height was worth 7.7 percent more than a slave who was one standard deviation shorter than the mean height. Some part of this increment in value may be because tall slaves were, on average, stronger, healthier, and more capable of intense labor than were short slaves. But two

[23] The Marine Society, the source of the height data on the London boys, was a charitable organization that received indigent or otherwise poor boys and prepared them for careers in the merchant marine or the Royal Navy.

[24] These Mississippi records were discovered by Armstead Robinson. The estimates of value appear to have been made by bona fide slave appraisers. The contraband sample is exceptional not only because of the information on value but also because it is a rare instance, for the early and mid-nineteenth century, when data are available for both height and weight. The Mississippi slaves had a mean weight of 2.3 pounds per inch of height, when measured at mean height. Corresponding figures for samples of adults aged thirty to thirty-four are 2.2 pounds per inch for whites in the Union Army, 2.3 pounds per inch for white registrants in World War II, and 2.3 pounds per inch for black registrants in World War II. These weight-by-height figures indicate that Mississippi slaves were slightly heavier, for given stature, than the whites in the Union Army but about the same as registrants for selective service in World War II. The Union Army figure was computed by fitting a linear regression to the data in the Gould report, 426–428; the World War II figures are from Karpinos (1958).

other factors, which could not be entered into the regression because of the absence of information on them in the contraband sample, are probably reflected in the differential in value, which was associated with stature. It is probable that healthy slaves had a longer life expectation than unhealthy ones. It is also possible that slaves in the more highly skilled jobs were taller than those engaged in field work. Thus the increase in productivity implied by the height differential in value could have taken several forms: one is greater intensity of labor per day at a given task and for a fixed expectation of life and labor; a second is unchanged intensity of daily labor at a given task with an increased expectation of life and labor; and a third is unchanged intensity of daily labor and life expectation but employment in occupations requiring greater skill than ordinary field work.

Analysis of the data in the Trinidad sample bears on these possibilities. Height was a factor in the selection of slaves for particular occupations in Trinidad. Among adult males, craftsmen were on average 0.5 inches taller and drivers (the foremen of field gangs) a full inch taller than field hands, whereas domestics were an inch shorter than field hands. Since slaves were not usually chosen for craft occupations until their twenties, and since regression analysis revealed no relationship between the occupation of the parents and the height of the children, it appears that the final height of children was not affected by their position but that owners or overseers used height as a criterion for determining which slaves would be assigned to particular occupations.

The most important result to emerge from the study of the Trinidad data thus far is that death did not choose slaves at random. Short slaves at every age during the life cycle were more likely to die than were tall ones. After standardizing for age, the annual death rate for the shortest quintile of males (forty-seven per one thousand) over a twenty-month period extending from 1813 to 1815 was more than twice as great as that of the tallest quintile of males (twenty-one per one thousand). Among females, the standardized death rates for the lowest and highest quintiles of height were forty-three and twenty-nine per one thousand, which suggests that female death rates were less sensitive to nutritional circumstances than were male death rates. One implication of this finding is that the combination of the exceedingly high death rates in Trinidad and the large impact of height on the probability of dying makes the observed height-by-age profile rise more rapidly than would have been so in a less severe environment, in which a larger proportion of short slaves would have survived to adult ages. Alternative simulations suggest that a 50 percent reduction in the death rate, with other factors held constant, might have reduced the observed final heights of males by approximately 1 inch.

## Some Economic and Demographic Issues

The apparent downward shift in the U.S. height profile for native-born whites during the last several decades of the antebellum era does not imply that the profile of every subpopulation declined: the decline might have been heavily concentrated within the urban population. The rate of urbanization accelerated sharply after 1820, and conditions of life in the larger cities apparently deteriorated. There is evidence in several northeastern cities of an upward trend in the mortality rates. Another possibility is that the decline was the consequence of an increased flow of immigrants; experiments on animals indicate that malnutrition in one generation affects the size of subsequent generations. The patterns observed in the height-by-age data are consistent with evidence that the period between 1820 and 1860 was marked by an increase in the inequality of income distribution, with the heights and wages of common laborers falling relative to those of other groups.[25]

The two cycles in height discovered for U.S. slaves probably have somewhat different explanations. Since the coastwise manifests did not distinguish between foreign- and native-born slaves, and given the 3-inch differential between the heights of U.S.-born and African-born slaves in Trinidad indicated by the data, an increase from 15 to 30 percent in the proportion of the African-born slaves listed in the manifests could account for about three-quarters of the first decline in slave heights. Since the years between the end of the Revolution and the close of the international slave trade witnessed a sharp increase in slave imports, such an explanation is plausible. Some part of the second height decline (that of slaves born in the late 1830s and the 1840s) might be due to ethnic mix, but it is unlikely that the share so attributed could exceed one-quarter of the estimated decline. The

---

[25] Yasuba (1962); Chandra (1975); Lindert and Williamson (1976).

Trinidad data indicate that the first generation of native-born males in nonsugar production were about 1.5 inches taller than the African-born males, which suggests that about half of the height gap was made up in one generation. Moreover, it is probable that close to half of the persons descended from Africans imported into the United States between 1783 and 1808 and born between 1835 and 1845 were not children but grandchildren or great-grandchildren of Africans. It seems likely, therefore, that most of the second decline was due to a rise in the intensity of labor, a decline in meat consumption, a rise in morbidity, or some combination of all these factors.[26]

The changing levels of nutrition and health over time implied by the height data have substantial implications for the study of the U.S. mortality experience. The evidently high level of nutrition in America at the time of the Revolution may well provide a partial explanation for the low mortality rates, relative to Europe, that characterized the early U.S. demographic experience. Because the consumption of food is a major component of the standard of living in preindustrial societies, the advantage in height also provides strong evidence of the superior material conditions enjoyed by the average American during the period. However, despite an apparently close correlation between changes in heights and mortality during the years between 1730 and 1850, a substantial portion of the pre-1850 decline in national mortality rates appears to be explained by factors other than changes in nutrition.[27]

---

[26] Steckel (1979). The estimated effects of ethnic mix on the cycles in slave heights should be considered upper bounds for two reasons. First, to the extent that imported slaves were West Indian creoles, the effect of changes in the ethnic mix on mean height would be diminished. Curtin's investigations suggest that about 90% of all slaves imported into the United States between 1701 and 1810 were born in Africa. Second, since the proportion of African-born slaves in the U.S. slave population between 1780 and 1810 appears to have varied in a relatively narrow range (18%–22%), a doubling of the proportion of African slaves among those born between 1775 and 1795 suggests sharp changes in the age structure of African imports, with the share of children rising more rapidly and reaching higher levels than has hitherto been supposed (Curtin 1969; Fogel and Engerman 1974; Galenson 1982).

[27] The height data will also be used to test the hypothesis that nutrition affected U.S. fertility rates. Recent summaries of evidence bearing on the link between nutrition, fecundity (reproductive capacity), and fertility (actual reproduction) are Bongaarts (1980) and Menken et al. (1981). Both articles stress that moderate chronic malnutrition has only "a minor effect on fecundity" and that the effect on fertility "is very small" (Bongaarts 1980, 568). However, famine and severe chronic malnutrition can substantially reduce fertility. It is not clear how much of the reduction associated with famine and severe chronic malnutrition is due to a decline in fecundity

The late eighteenth and early nineteenth centuries were character-ized by the narrowing of interregional differences in mortality rates between New England and the South. Crude mortality rates in Mas-sachusetts appear to have remained in the fifteen to twenty-five per one thousand range throughout this period, while the rates for whites in the South declined from about fifty to about twenty-five per one thou-sand. The higher mean final height found for the South than for the North during this period tends to dispel the notion that the southern mortality rates were linked to lower levels of nutrition in that area. It now seems more likely that superior nutritional circumstances oper-ated to close the gap between regional death rates by counteracting factors that increased mortality in the South (disease pool, climate, etc.). Fragmentary evidence suggests that southerners were heavy con-sumers of meat in the late colonial and early national eras.[28]

Nevertheless, it is possible that some part of the height advantage of the South was due to the Trinidad effect. Although death rates were far less severe in the South between 1750 and 1860 than in Trinidad circa 1813, the higher probability of death for shorter persons would have inflated southern heights relative to northern ones, over and above the direct nutritional effect. Consequently, there appears to be not only a direct nutritional effect but also (holding nutrition constant) a mortality effect and an interaction effect. The magnitudes of these separate effects are yet to be determined.[29]

---

(although amenorrhea and reduction in sperm motility and longevity are involved) and how much is due to such indirect factors as loss of libido, increased separation of spouses (because of search for work or food), and, especially for societies during the eighteenth and nineteenth centuries, increases in deaths, which led to a premature ending of childbearing or to increased birth intervals (because widowhood reduces sexual intercourse) (cf. Frisch 1978; NBER 1980).

[28] Gray (1933); Vinovskis (1972); Fogel et al. (1978); Sokoloff and Villaflor (1982). In 1901, the earliest year for which systematic surveys of food consumption by region are available, the per capita consumption of beef and pork was about 4% greater in the South than in the North. The food survey is from the U.S. Bureau of Labor (1903). The North is an average of the North Atlantic and North Central regions, and the South is an average of the South Atlantic and South Central regions, using the regional populations as weights.

[29] The Trinidad effect might also have contributed to the decline in white heights after the mid-1820s, shown in Figure 2.3, since persons from the earlier birth cohorts who survived to be mustered into the Union Army would be taller than those from later birth cohorts, even if the mean height of each cohort at a specified age (such as thirty) was the same. Given the prevailing mortality schedules, however, and the age span

We are, as previously indicated, studying the relationship between mortality and nutrition in the United States (using height as an index of nutrition), and we are also introducing measures of nutritional status into production functions for both the agricultural and manufacturing sectors. The results of the latter procedure may not be unambiguous because the intensification of labor that enhanced productivity and accompanied the growth of the manufacturing sector could have led to an increase in the per capita energy output relative to the consumption of calories and nutrients among adolescent laborers, and this may have produced a decline in stature.

It cannot be assumed, therefore, that a decrease in the final heights of native-born whites after 1825 necessarily implies a reduction in per capita food consumption. It might seem unlikely that the stature of whites, who were free and who experienced most of their growth by age twenty, would be much influenced by changes in labor organization. During the nineteenth century, however, especially before 1850, boys commonly entered the labor force before age sixteen, which generally preceded the peak of the adolescent growth spurt. Consequently, a decline in height could have resulted because there was an increase in the per capita energy output of these young workers without a corresponding increase in the per capita consumption of calories and nutrients. British investigations of child labor in factories during the nineteenth century support this hypothesis. Children of a given socioeconomic class who worked in factories were substantially shorter at each age than children of the same class who were not so employed.[30]

Still, it is possible that the food consumption of the urban laboring classes did decline between 1825 and 1860. This possibility cannot be ruled out either because of the slight downward trend in food prices or because of the upward trend in some of the currently available indexes of real wages. Part of the problem with the wage indexes, as previously noted, is that the series on money wages may confound urban with rural wage rates and is not adequately standardized for a locational and occupational mix. Another part of the problem is that

---

involved (twenty-five to forty-five), the Trinidad effect could account for only about one-tenth of the drop after the mid-1820s, shown in Figure 2.3, and it could not explain the preceding rise in heights.

[30] Great Britain (1833); British Association for the Advancement of Science (1884).

the current measures of consumer prices do not include data on the cost of shelter, which may have accounted for a quarter or more of the total expenditures of urban laborers during this period. There is considerable evidence that the rapid growth of the urban population between 1820 and 1860 led to severe shortages in urban housing and hence probably to a sharp rise in the price of shelter. The decline in the availability of wood and the shift from wood to coal as a fuel source may also have contributed to the rising cost of shelter.

Consequently, it is entirely possible that an index of consumer prices that included the cost of shelter would show a decline in the real wages of urban laborers between 1825 and 1860. Moreover, if the income and price elasticities of the demand for shelter by urban laborers (at the relatively meager incomes of the time) were sufficiently low, sharp rises in the cost of shelter could have led to decreases in the amount of food consumed, particularly in the consumption of such relatively expensive foods as meat and fish, even in the face of constant or declining food prices.

In the English case, we have been able to make a comparison between a series on heights and a widely used series on real wages for London artisans. Although Von Tunzelmann has demonstrated that nationwide indexes of real wages are unreliable because of the implicit shifts in the weights brought about by the splicing together of diverse series, the question remains as to whether indexes for particular localities and classes of labor are reliable. Also at issue is the assumption that trends in the real wages of artisans mirror those of common laborers. Tucker's series on the real wages of London artisans benefits from the restriction of its geographical scope to one locality. When one compares the mean height of boys between the ages of fourteen and sixteen from families of common laborers in the London area, over the years between 1775 and 1865, with Tucker's series, a certain degree of conformity is evident (see Figure 2.4). The heights of the boys will reflect their cumulative nutritional experience over their lifetimes, and especially the experience of the years immediately preceding and during the growth spurt. Accordingly, the height series is related to the wage series lagged five years, although longer lags (ten and thirteen years) provide similar results.[31]

---

[31] Each observation is an average of ten years centered at the indicated date (Von Tunzelmann 1979).

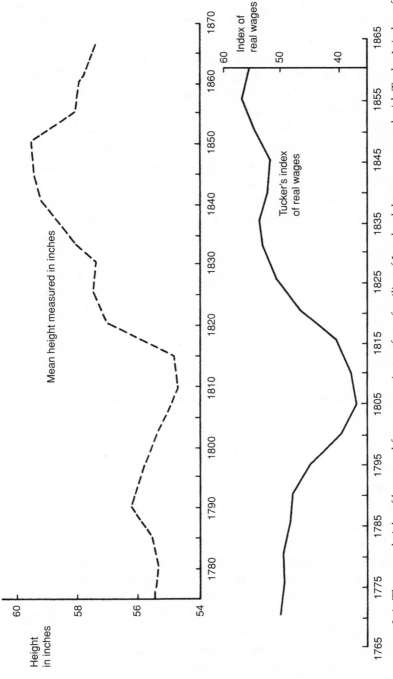

FIGURE 2.4. The mean height of boys aged fourteen to sixteen from families of London laborers compared with Tucker's index of the real wage of London artisans, 1770–1865. *Source:* Preliminary sample of Marine Society ($N = 37,957$) (Tucker 1975).

The two series generally move together during both rising and declining phases, except for the last two decades. The correlation suggests that for most of the century, the real wages of artisans and of the poorest sections of the London working class tended to move together. However, the elasticity of height with respect to Tucker's wage index is not constant, and the preliminary regression analysis of the relationship between the height of boys in the Marine Society and the occupational strata within the laboring classes changed over time. These findings raise the possibility of a changing relationship between the wages of common laborers and of artisans even prior to 1840 and illustrate the problem of generalizing from the experience of one group of a population (or the average) to the experiences of other groups.

During the past half century, economic and social historians have developed new measures, such as per capita income and indexes of real wages, that have shed much light on the course of economic development and on the degree to which various socioeconomic classes have shared in the benefits of that development. Use of these measures has helped to correct misimpressions that were based on isolated scraps of evidence, but such use has also raised new questions that reveal the limitation of these measures. For many countries, reliable per capita income estimates could not be pushed back much further than the mid-nineteenth century and then could only be constructed for decadal intervals. Consequently, national income accounts have shed relatively little light on the evolution of cyclical phenomena or on how and when differences in per capita income among nations, which were already large by 1850 or 1860, came into being. Similar problems have arisen with long-term series of real wages, which are often spliced together from a variety of short series in the hope that shifting from one occupation to another, or one locality to another, would not undermine the comparability of the observations in the series.

Efforts to fill existing gaps in knowledge have taken many directions, and the exploration of the uses of data on height is one of them. Those data on height contain much information on economic and social well-being and comprise one of the oldest propositions in the social sciences. Such distinguished figures of the past two centuries as Louis René Villerme in France, Adolphe Quetelet in Belgium, Edwin Chadwick and Francis Galton in England, and Benjamin A. Gould and Franz Boas in the United States have used this body of information to investigate economic and social behavior. Recent efforts are therefore not breaking with scientific tradition but are returning to a fruitful line of research with larger and richer data sets, improved statistical techniques, and the expanded capacity to handle large data sets, which has been made possible by high-speed computers.

The preliminary findings of the new work are promising, but the tentative nature of the findings should be emphasized. The most secure generalization to emerge so far is that patterns of improvement in nutrition and health after 1700 were more varied and complex than is usually appreciated. Although heights and nutrition appear to have improved markedly in the United States (and the colonies that preceded it) during the eighteenth century, so that modern heights were reached by the time of the American Revolution, similar developments in Western Europe were delayed by as much as a century. England appears to have been at least a half century into its Industrial Revolution before witnessing a marked improvement in the heights or nutrition of its laboring classes. Down to the end of the Napoleonic wars, the nutritional levels of poor London adolescents were worse than they are today in all but a few of the most impoverished populations of the underdeveloped world.

Nutritional advances during the nineteenth century were uneven both among different classes within particular nations and across the nations of the North Atlantic community. In the United States, the height differentials between socioeconomic classes were markedly greater during the Civil War than they had been during the Revolution. In England, however, the growth profile of the London poor shifted upward so rapidly that half of the gap with modern teenage heights was closed in just two or three decades. Increases in average height were not as continuous as has often been supposed in either Europe or America but were interrupted by substantial periods of decline. In the American case, average heights of both whites and blacks began to decline with cohorts born during the late 1820s or early 1830s and continued to do so past the Civil War. Rapid and sustained increases in height probably resumed with cohorts born some time before World War I and proceeded, at rates outstripping previous experience, for half a century.

What is at issue now is the explanation for these patterns of change in heights and nutrition. Among the factors that might be involved are changes in the ethnic composition of the native-born population, increased claims on food intake as a consequence of increased intensity of labor or a deteriorating disease environment, and shifts in the urban–rural composition of the population. The life cycle and intergenerational data sets now being linked to the height-by-age data should help to differentiate among these possibilities as well as to determine the effects of changes in nutrition during the growing ages on labor productivity, morbidity, and mortality at later stages of the life cycle.

# 3

## Second Thoughts on the European Escape from Hunger

### *Famines, Chronic Malnutrition, and Mortality Rates*

Most of the people in the world are poor, so if we knew the economics of being poor we would know much of the economics that really matters.
– T. W. Schultz (1980)

During the late 1960s, a wide consensus emerged among social and economic historians regarding the causes of the decline in the high European death rates that prevailed at the beginning of the early modern era. The high average mortality rates of the years preceding the vital revolution were attributed to periodic mortality crises that raised normal mortality rates by 50 to 100 percent or more. It was the elimination of these peaks, rather than the lowering of the plateau of mortality in normal years, that was believed to be principally responsible for the much lower mortality rates that prevailed at the end of the nineteenth century (Helleiner 1964; Wrigley 1969; Flinn 1970). These crises, it was held, were precipitated either by acute harvest failures or by epidemics (Flinn 1970). Some scholars argued that even if the diseases were not nutritionally sensitive, famines played a major role because epidemics were spread by the beggars who swarmed from one place to another in search of food (Meuvert 1965). Whatever the differences on this issue, it was widely agreed that many of the mortality crises were due to starvation brought on by harvest failure (Wrigley 1969; Flinn 1970, 1974).

A mechanism by which a harvest failure was transformed into a mortality crisis was proposed by Hoskins in two influential papers

39

published in the 1960s (Hoskins 1964, 1968). Noting that it was possible to identify harvest failures by looking at the deviations in grain prices from their normal level, Hoskins computed the annual deviations of wheat prices from a thirty-one-year moving average of these prices. Normal harvests were defined as those with prices that were within ±10 percent of the trend. He found that over the 280 years from 1480 to 1759, good harvests (prices 10% or more below trends) were about 50 percent more frequent than deficient harvests (prices 10% or more above trends). His most important finding, however, was that good and bad harvests (as shown by prices) ran in sequences, so there were frequently three or four bad years in a row. These sequences, he argued, were due primarily not to weather cycles but to the low yield-to-seed ratios, which he put at about 4 or 5 for wheat at the beginning of the sixteenth century. Thus one bad harvest tended to generate another because starving farmers consumed their reserve for seeds. The consequence of several bad harvests in a row was a mortality crisis.

The interpretation of the European escape from hunger and high death rates embodied in this train of research was brought into question with the publication of *The Population History of England, 1541–1871: A Reconstruction*, by E. A. Wrigley and R. S. Schofield (1981). Using data from 404 parish registers widely distributed throughout England, these scholars and their associates constructed monthly and annual estimates of the English population over a 331-year period as well as monthly and annual estimates of the national birthrates, mortality rates, and nuptial rates. Although important issues have been raised about various assumptions employed in the analytical procedures that transformed the information on baptisms and burials contained in the Anglican registers into national estimates of birthrates and death rates, it is widely agreed that the reconstruction was carried out with meticulous care and that the various adjustments for deficiencies in the record were judicious. Whatever the shortcomings of the reconstructions, the new time series produced by Wrigley and Schofield have become the foundation for all further research into the demographic history of England (Flinn 1982; Lindert 1983).

In addition to presenting their basic time series and describing the complex procedures employed to produce them, Wrigley and

Schofield began the processes of relating these demographic rates to underlying economic and social phenomena. They determined that both fertility rates and marriage rates were strongly correlated with measures of real wages and the cost of living but that mortality rates were not.[1] A chapter of the book contributed by Lee (1981) reported a statistically significant but weak relationship between short-term variations in death rates and in wheat prices, but Lee, as well as Wrigley and Schofield, concluded that short-run variations in English mortality were "overwhelmingly determined" by factors other than the food supply (Schofield 1983). Insofar as the long-term trend in mortality was concerned, Wrigley and Schofield reported that they were unable to find even a weak statistical correlation between mortality rates and the food supply (Wrigley and Schofield 1981).

Since the findings of Wrigley, Schofield, and Lee appear to be so sharply in conflict with the train of research that has linked the escape from high mortality rates to the escape from hunger, it is tempting to declare that one of the research trains must be wrong and to choose sides. I believe that such a conclusion is not only premature but very likely wrong. The aim of this chapter is to reconsider the older line of research in the light of the findings of Wrigley, Schofield, and Lee to see where they are compatible and where the evidence tilts toward one or the other side.

In the next section, I present evidence indicating that the elimination of crisis mortality accounted for only a small part of the decline in national mortality rates during the nineteenth century. The third section argues that some previous attempts to infer the extent of the shortfall in the quantity of foodgrains harvested from movements of prices have exaggerated that shortfall because of overestimates of the elasticity of demand for foodgrains. The fourth section presents an alternative hypothesis that makes sharp changes in the distribution of foodgrains, resulting from relatively small shortfalls in output, the principal cause of periodic famines. A mechanism underlying such

---

[1] The analysis of Wrigley and Schofield is cast in terms of crude death rates rather than age-standardized rates because the counts of vital events in their 404 parishes do not give the specific ages at which these events occurred; consequently, they were not able to examine the effects of famines on the age structure of mortality.

distributional changes is proposed. It is then argued in the fifth section that famines could have been avoided, and apparently were avoided, during 1600–1640 in England by proper government policies. The next section deals with the effects of chronic malnutrition on mortality rates. It presents evidence that suggests that most of the secular decline in mortality in England, France, and Sweden before 1875, and about half of the decline between 1875 and 1975, was due to the reduction of chronic malnutrition. The seventh section presents the principal findings of the chapter and briefly comments on their implications for current debates on policy.

One of the most important aspects of *The Population History* is the new light it sheds on mortality crises over the 331 years it covers. Wrigley and Schofield are the first scholars who have had a sample of parishes large enough in number and wide enough in geographic coverage to permit an estimate of the national impact of mortality crises on the annual crude death rates in early modern England. Following established procedures, they measure mortality crises as deviations from a twenty-five-year moving average and define a crisis year as one with an annual crude death rate (CDR) that is more than 10 percent above trend. That criterion yielded forty-five crisis years, a bit less than 14 percent of the years in their study (Wrigley and Schofield 1981). They also computed national crisis months (months with monthly death rates at least 25% above trend) and found that ninety-four years contained at least one such crisis month.[2] Their analysis confirmed many of the findings of scholars working with less complete data. The year 1558–1559, for example, emerged as by far the worst year for mortality in the entire period. They also found that the most severe mortality crises were concentrated during 1544–1658, although there was a lethal recurrence during the late 1720s.

Perhaps the most important aspect of the new time series on mortality, however, is that these data drastically diminish the role of crisis mortality as an explanation for the high mortality rates that generally prevailed between 1541 and 1800. This conclusion emerges from two tables in *The Population History*, which together provide the data

[2] See Wrigley and Schofield (1981), pp. 338–339.

needed to compute the crisis component of total mortality. The results of the computation are presented in Table 3.1 by quarter centuries (or fractions thereof) as well as by centuries (or fractions thereof). In no quarter century did crisis mortality account for as much as 10 percent of the total mortality. Even after crisis mortality is factored out, the normal mortality remains above twenty-five per thousand for the sixteenth, seventeenth, and eighteenth centuries. Indeed, the normal mortality rate of the eighteenth century was as high as the total mortality rate of each of the two preceding centuries, despite their many crises. Consequently, the escape from high mortality rates was due primarily not to the elimination of crises, as many have previously argued, but to the reduction in so-called normal mortality levels. Nearly three-quarters of the decline of mortality between 1726–1750 and 1851–1871, despite the relatively high level of crisis mortality at the beginning of this period and its negligible level at the end of it, was due to the reduction of normal mortality.

It follows that, even if every national mortality crisis identified by Wrigley and Schofield was the result of a famine, the elimination of periodic famines cannot be the principal explanation for the secular morality. This is not to deny that famines in particular localities at particular times produced great increases in local mortality rates: too much evidence of local disasters induced by food shortages has accumulated to rule out such phenomena. However, in light of the Wrigley–Schofield data, it now seems clear that, dramatic as they were, mortality crises, whether caused by famines or not, were too scattered in time and space to have been the principal factor in the secular decline in mortality after 1540.[3]

*The Population History* does not provide the same challenge to previous thought on the scope of subsistence crises as it does on the question of mortality crises. Indeed, the periods that Wrigley and Schofield identified as the major subsistence crises (Wrigley and Schofield 1981) generally coincide with those identified by Hoskins (1964). That

---

[3] It is, however, still possible that mortality crises were a much larger part of total mortality before 1541 than they were afterward, both because of differences in the nature of the prevailing diseases in the two periods and because food supplies were probably more inadequate in medieval times.

TABLE 3.1. *The Impact of Crisis Mortality on the Average Crude Death Rate: England, 1541–1871*

| Period | -1 CDR per 1,000 Person-Years | -2 Crisis Mortality per 1,000 Person-Years | -3 CDR after Factoring out Crisis Mortality (per 1,000) | -4 Crisis Mortality as % of Average Mortality | -5 Crisis Mortality as % of "Premature" Mortality |
|---|---|---|---|---|---|
| By quarter centuries | | | | | |
| (1) 1541–1550 | 30.33 | 2.25 | 28.08 | 7.42 | 9.64 |
| (2) 1551–1575 | 28.28 | 2.35 | 25.93 | 8.31 | 11.04 |
| (3) 1576–1600 | 24.21 | 1.22 | 22.99 | 5.04 | 7.09 |
| (4) 1601–1625 | 24.61 | 2.05 | 22.56 | 8.33 | 11.64 |
| (5) 1626–1650 | 26.36 | 0.99 | 25.37 | 3.76 | 5.11 |
| (6) 1651–1675 | 28.07 | 1.58 | 26.49 | 5.63 | 7.5 |
| (7) 1676–1700 | 30.29 | 1.66 | 28.63 | 5.48 | 7.13 |
| (8) 1701–1725 | 27.79 | 0.06 | 27.73 | 0.22 | 0.29 |
| (9) 1726–1750 | 30.57 | 2.34 | 28.23 | 6.4 | 9.93 |
| (10) 1751–1775 | 27.28 | 0.4 | 26.88 | 1.47 | 1.97 |
| (11) 1776–1800 | 26.85 | 0.55 | 26.3 | 2.05 | 2.77 |
| (12) 1801–1825 | 25.4 | 0.15 | 25.25 | 0.59 | 0.82 |
| (13) 1826–1850 | 22.58 | 0.13 | 22.45 | 0.58 | 0.83 |
| (14) 1851–1871 | 22.42 | 0.13 | 22.29 | 0.58 | 0.84 |

By centuries

| | Col. 1 | Col. 2 | Col. 3 | Col. 4 | Col. 5 |
|---|---|---|---|---|---|
| (15) 1541–1600 | 26.93 | 1.87 | 25.06 | 6.92 | 9.38 |
| (16) 1601–1700 | 27.33 | 1.57 | 25.76 | 5.74 | 7.72 |
| (17) 1701–1800 | 28.12 | 0.83 | 27.29 | 2.95 | 3.93 |
| (18) 1801–1871 | 23.53 | 0.14 | 23.39 | 0.59 | 0.85 |

*Notes:* Lines 1–4, Col. 1: Each entry is the average of the quinquennial rates for the period given in Wrigley and Schofield (1981). Col. 2: Each entry is the difference between the corresponding entries in cols. 1 and 3. Col. 3: Wrigley and Schofield (1981) give the CDR ($D_{cc}$) for each of the forty-five years they identify as a crisis year as well as the percentage deviation of the crisis CDR from a twenty-five-year moving average, which is taken to be the normal CDR for that year. Hence, by dividing 1 plus the percentage deviation into the crisis CDR, it is possible to obtain the normal CDR for the crisis year ($D_{nc}$). It is also possible to solve the following equation for normal CDR in noncrisis year ($D_{nn}$):

$$D = \theta D_{cc} + (1 - \theta) D_{nn},$$

where $D$ is the average CDR for the time period (as shown in col. 1) and $\theta$ is the share of crisis years during the time period. The average CDR with the crisis mortality factored out ($D_n$) is then given by

$$D_n = \theta D_{nc} + (1 - \theta) D_{nn}.$$

The entries in col. 3 are the values of $D_n$. Col. 4: Each entry is 1 minus the ratio of the col. 3 entry to the col. 1 entry.

Lines 15–18, Cols. 1 and 3: The entries for each period are an average of the corresponding figures for the subperiods in lines 1–14, weighted by the number of years in the subperiods. Col. 2: Each entry is the difference between the corresponding entries in cols. 1 and 3. Col. 4: Each entry is 1 minus the ratio of the col. 3 entry to the col. 1 entry. Col. 5: "Premature" mortality is defined as the crude death rate of 1980 standardized for the English age structure of 1701–1705 (see Fogel 1986b, table 1).

TABLE 3.2. *A Comparison between King's Law and a Constant Elasticity of Demand Equation*

| King's Law | | $Q = 1.00P^{-0.403}$ | |
|---|---|---|---|
| Q | P | Q | P |
| 1.0 | 1.0 | 1.00 | 1.0 |
| 0.9 | 1.3 | 0.90 | 1.3 |
| 0.8 | 1.8 | 0.79 | 1.8 |
| 0.7 | 2.6 | 0.68 | 2.6 |
| 0.6 | 3.8 | 0.58 | 3.8 |
| 0.5 | 5.5 | 0.50 | 5.5 |

*Note:* 1 = normal price and yield.
*Source:* Slicher Van Bath (1963) presents King's law and compares it with those of Jevons and Bouniatian.

outcome is not surprising because the procedures used in the iden-tification and measurement of subsistence crises by Wrigley, Schofield, and Lee are quite similar to those of Hoskins. Wrigley and Schofield used annual deviations in an index of real wages from a twenty-five-year trend to identify subsistence crises. Because of the procedure for smoothing the wage series, as they pointed out, nearly all the variabil-ity in the index came from the price deflator, which was dominated by grains (broadly defined). Lee, like Hoskins, relied on wheat prices alone, on the grounds that the price of wheat was so highly correlated with other food prices that wheat was "a good proxy for food prices in general" (Lee 1981, 357).

The tradition of judging the shortfall in the food supply by price is an ancient one dating back at least to Gregory King, who first formalized the systematic relationship between the yield of a harvest and the subsequent price of the grain. Called *King's law*, his schema (see Table 3.2) has been employed as an estimate of the elasticity of demand for wheat. Later economists, such as Jevons and Bouniatian, formulated quite similar laws in equations (Slicher Van Bath 1963). All three laws are closely approximated by constant elasticity demand curves, with $\varepsilon$ ranging between 0.403 and 0.422. As Table 3.2 shows, the equation

$$Q = 1.00P^{-0.403} \tag{1}$$

gives a very close fit to King's law in the specified range of prices.[4]
It seems quite reasonable, therefore, to use the deviation in price to
infer the deviation in the yield of a harvest from its normal level, as
numerous analysts have done ever since King's time.

When King's law is combined with the proposition that the yield-
to-seed ratio of wheat was about 4 – that is, that one-quarter of the
crop was needed for seeds – the interpretation of harvest failures
developed from price series by Hoskins and numerous other scholars during the past three decades follows immediately. Wheat prices
50 percent above normal imply a harvest that is 15 percent below
normal, a situation presumed to have put heavy pressure on farmers to dip into their seed reserves. With two such years in a row,
even if farmers succeeded in maintaining the normal proportion of
the crop for seed reserves, consumption in the second year would be
cut by more than a quarter, pushing the average food intake of the
lower classes to perhaps 1,340 calories per equivalent adult or less per
day.[5] How devastating, then, must have been years such as 1555 and
1556, when a 51 percent deviation of the price of wheat above normal
was followed by a 105 percent deviation above normal, suggesting
a decline of lower-class consumption to the neighborhood of 1,180
calories.[6]

---

[4] In a constant elasticity demand equation of the form $Q = DP^{-\varepsilon}$, $D$ represents all of
the variables that might cause the intercept of demand curve to shift (income, prices
of substitutes, prices of complements). The implicit assumption of those who have
used King's law is that both $D$ and $\varepsilon$ are constant. When all variables are standardized
on 1, $D = 1$. It should also be kept in mind that in applications of King's law,
wheat is generally used as a proxy for grain or food. Since applications of King's law
generally do not take account of the possibility that $\varepsilon$ shifted during periods of dearth,
I have worked within the framework of that tradition in this section because my aim
here is to reveal issues that do not turn on a shifting demand curve. In the fourth
section, an adjustment is made for a shifting elasticity. However, in both sections, it
is assumed that the aggregate demand curve is relatively fixed and that year-to-year
fluctuations in price are due primarily to shifts in a perfectly inelastic short-run supply
curve from one harvest to another. See the appendix for a further discussion of these
points.

[5] The figure on caloric consumption is derived by applying $(1.5^{-0.403})^2$ to the average
caloric consumption of the three lowest deciles of the English distribution in Table
3.8.

[6] The figure is derived in the same way as in Note 5, except that the factor is $(1.51^{-0.403})$
$(2.05^{-0.403})$.

The problem is that the implied level of caloric consumption in 1556 is too low to be believable because it is well below the requirement for basal metabolism. We know, both from controlled semistarvation experiments and from actual conditions in underdeveloped countries today, that even levels of 1,300–1,500 calories produce protein-energy malnutrition (PEM) serious enough to incapacitate a large proportion of the population and also lead to so many cases of kwashiorkor that death rates increase significantly among those affected (Scrimshaw 1987; De Maeyer 1976; Mellor and Gavian 1987; Kumar 1987; Foreign Office Commission 1985). A population forced to consume less than basal metabolism for a whole year would have produced noticeable increases in mortality. Yet the Wrigley–Schofield time series, while confirming Hoskins' finding that 1555 and 1556 were years of extreme dearth, reports that the mortality rates during these two years averaged about 10 percent below normal (Wrigley and Schofield 1981). Indeed, after searching for a correlation between extreme annual deviations in prices and in mortality rates, they concluded that no significant contemporaneous relationship existed, although there was evidence of a weak lagged relationship.[7]

This puzzle is not necessarily without a solution. One possibility is that government intervention prevented a subsistence crisis from turning into a mortality crisis. (Some questions about the role of the government will be explored in the fifth section.) Another possibility is that defects in the Wrigley–Schofield estimates of mortality may explain the anomalous results. Yet their ingenious procedures for correcting the undercount of deaths, if less than perfect, seem to have produced a series quite adequate for the particular analysis they have undertaken. The problem, I believe, lies not so much in the data but in a series of implicit assumptions that have gradually crept into the analysis of the data, assumptions made so often that they have hardened into an unquestioned procedure. It was only with the discovery of the Wrigley–Schofield paradox that the need to reconsider the analytical procedures became evident.

---

[7] See Wrigley and Schofield (1981) pp. 325–326. Lee, in his 1981 study (379–382) and in a letter to me (dated July 10, 1989), has pointed out that his analysis of the correlation between wheat prices and morality revealed a strong simultaneous relationship in the 9 years (out of 287) that the proportional deviation of wheat prices from their trend exceeded two standard deviations (cf. Fogel 1986a, 494–495, 524n46).

The crux of the problem lies with the application of King's law, which, as has been indicated, is well described by a simple demand equation of the form

$$Q = P^{-\varepsilon}. \tag{2}$$

When $P$ (price) and $Q$ (quantity) are measured as proportional deviations from trend, (2) becomes

$$\overset{*}{Q} = -\varepsilon \overset{*}{P}, \tag{3}$$

where an asterisk over a variable indicates percentage deviations from trend and $\varepsilon$ is the elasticity of demand. Equation (3), which is the definition of that elasticity, is thus a simple linear equation in which the value of the coefficient of the right-hand variable is given by

$$\varepsilon = \frac{\sigma_q}{\sigma_p} r_{pq} = \frac{\overset{*}{Q}}{\overset{*}{P}}, \tag{4}$$

where $\sigma_q$ is the standard deviation (s.d.) of $\overset{*}{Q}$, $\sigma_p$ is the s.d. of $\overset{*}{P}$, and $r_{pq}$ is the correlation coefficient between $\overset{*}{Q}$ and $\overset{*}{P}$. It follows that the value of $\varepsilon$ will be greatest when $r_{pq}$ is assumed to equal 1, which is the assumption generally made in the application of King's law. Because this assumption is not at issue in the analysis that follows, and because a value of $r_{pq}$ less than 1 would strengthen my argument, I will assume that $r_{pq} = 1$ in the balance of the discussion.

It follows from (4) that one can estimate an elasticity for wheat by obtaining estimates of $\sigma_p$ and $\sigma_q$. The estimate of $\sigma_p$ for wheat is readily available from the wheat prices used by Lee and is about 0.22 for the period 1540–1840 (Lee 1981, 374). The value of $\sigma_q$ (measured as a proportional deviation from trend), computed for the first thirty years for which data on the physical yield of wheat in England are available (1884–1913), is 0.040.[8] Assuming, as a first approximation,

---

[8] The implicit assumption in the literature is that acres planted remained constant and that net imports were zero so that all of the yearly variation in the quantity of grain was due to variation in yields. To avoid complicating the argument further than need be, I have accepted these assumptions. The effect of the assumptions is to bias the result against the point I am making since the root mean squared errors (RMSEs) around the trend of total production and around the trend of total production plus imports were below the RMSE around the trend of yield during 1884–1913.

that the climatic factors affecting the variability of yield were similar between the seventeenth century and the end of the nineteenth, the preceding figures imply that the demand elasticity for wheat was 0.183 (0.0402/0.220), which is more than 50 percent below the elasticity of the demand for wheat implied by King's law, or at least by the way that it has been interpreted.[9]

The problem with some previous interpretations of King's law is that investigators implicitly assumed that carry-over stocks of wheat from the previous harvests were nil. This assumption was an unintended but necessary consequence of treating the deviations from normal annual yields (column 1 of Table 3.2) as the total supply – as when I used the series in columns 1 and 2 of that table to estimate Equation (1). However, the annual supply is not just the harvest in a given year but the harvest plus the carry-over stock from previous years. Davenant (1699) estimated that in normal times, carry-over stocks varied between four and five months (i.e., between 33% and 42% of a normal crop). Consequently, when estimating the demand curve, the proper quantity is not $Q$ but $Q'$ or $Q''$ (Table 3.3). When those series are substituted for $Q$, the estimated values are given by

$$Q' = 1.00 p^{-0.248} \quad \text{(when carry-overs are five months)} \quad (2a)$$

$$Q'' = 1.00 p^{-0.272} \quad \text{(when carry-overs are four months)} \quad (2b)$$

Thus, when one corrects for the neglect of carry-over stocks, King's law implies an elasticity of demand that is not only between 33 and 38 percent below the level often presumed but also a good deal closer to the estimate obtained by using the standard deviation of proportional

[9] Is it valid to use data for 1884–1913 to estimate the variability of per acre yields in the eighteenth century in view of the marked advances in agricultural technology after 1700? That point needs to be pursued, and it may be possible to estimate the average variance in annual per acre yields for the eighteenth century from data in estate records. One of the earliest time series is for the United States, which began its system of crop reporting shortly after the American Civil War. These data suggest that although the technological advances produced large increases in the average yield per acre, they had little effect on the coefficient of variation. For example, the mean wheat yield in the United States during 1961–1970 was more than twice the figure for 1871–1880; however, the coefficients of variation for the two time periods were virtually identical (computed from U.S. Bureau of the Census 1975). Despite irrigation, crop spraying, etc., the principal factors that affect variations around trend (e.g., rainfall, sunshine, temperature) do not seem, even today, to have yielded much to science.

TABLE 3.3. *The Effect of Allowing for Carry-Over Stocks in the Supply of Wheat at the End of the New Harvest*

| (1) Derivation from Normal Yield of Current Harvest $Q_j$ | (2) Price | (3) Deviation from Normal Supply if Carry-Over Is 5 months $Q'$ | (4) Deviation from Normal Supply If Carry-Over Is 4 Months $Q''$ |
|---|---|---|---|
| 1.0 | 1.0 | 1.00 | 1.00 |
| 0.9 | 1.3 | 0.93 | 0.92 |
| 0.8 | 1.8 | 0.86 | 0.85 |
| 0.7 | 2.6 | 0.79 | 0.78 |
| 0.6 | 3.8 | 0.72 | 0.70 |
| 0.5 | 5.5 | 0.65 | 0.62 |

*Note:* Cols. 1 and 2 are from Table 3.2; cols. 3 and 4 are computed from

$$Q_j^i = \theta I + (1 - \theta)Q_j,$$

where $I$ is the carry-over inventory, which is assumed to be constant for each value of $Q_j$ (taken from col. 1) and $\theta$ is the share of carry-over inventories after the close of a normal harvest ( $\theta = 0.294$ with 5-month carry-over and 0.250 with 4-month carry-over).

deviations of physical yields from trend at the end of the nineteenth century.

Before pursuing the implications of this finding, one other implicit assumption needs to be made explicit. This stems from the neglect of grains fed to livestock as a reserve for human consumption. Although the feeding off of grasses, clover, vetches, turnips, lentils, other meadow crops, and hay provided the bulk of animal feed, Davenant (1699) estimated that about 12 percent of annual grain production was normally fed to livestock. In other words, human consumption of grains (see Table 3.4) normally constituted only about 45 percent of the available supply at the close of a harvest. Even if we add the 17.6 percent reserved for seeds, there was still normally a reserve of 37.9 percent (carry-over plus feed) that could serve as a buffer before a deficient harvest required a restriction of human consumption on the seed reserve.

It follows from (3) that not even a 100 percent deviation of wheat price above trend, which occurred only once in the entire period examined by Hoskins, implied a physical shortfall of wheat (standing here for a typical grain) so large as to eliminate carry-over stocks, let alone

TABLE 3.4. *The Normal Distribution of the Supply of Grain (New Crop Plus Carry-Over Inventories) at the Close of Harvest*

|     |                       | %    |
| --- | --------------------- | ---- |
| (1) | Carry-over stocks     | 29.4 |
| (2) | Animal feed           | 8.5  |
| (3) | Seed for the next crop | 17.6 |
| (4) | Human consumption     | 44.5 |

*Source:* Lines 1 and 2, Davenant (1699); line 3, Hoskins (1968).

the combination of carry-over stocks and animal feed. Even the worst pair of years identified by Hoskins (1555 and 1556) would still have left more than 10 percent of the normal carry-over inventory as a buffer without encroaching on feed, seed, or human consumption in either year.[10]

The point of the preceding exercise is that even for a single grain, and even assuming a low yield-to-seed ratio, the physical shortfall in the worst pair of years was not so great as to require a general encroachment on seeds to maintain human consumption, although such encroachments undoubtedly occurred in some localities in some years, especially among the poorer farmers. This is not to say that the high prices did not cause sharp reductions in consumption, especially among the lower classes, or to deny the existence of famines. I mean only to call into question the proposition that *nationwide* subsistence crises after 1541 were the consequence of natural disasters.

Indeed, even the preceding discussion overemphasizes the part played by natural factors, since until now, I have accepted the common assumption that because wheat prices were highly correlated with other food prices, wheat prices alone are an acceptable proxy for an index of all food prices. However, when one is attempting to infer the variability of the quantity of food from the variability in wheat prices, the critical question is not the strength of the correlation but the size

---

[10] I do not mean to suggest that farmers actually dipped deeply into carry-over inventories or into feed stores when grain prices rose. Indeed, as I shall argue later, they were quite unwilling to do so. Nevertheless, those inventories were more than adequate to cover the food needs of the destitute without encroaching on reserves for seeds.

of the elasticity between these two variables. Since the elasticity ($\alpha$) of all food prices with respect to wheat prices is given by

$$\frac{\overset{*}{P}_f}{\overset{*}{P}_w} = \alpha = \frac{\sigma_f}{\sigma_w} r_{fw}, \tag{5}$$

it follows that if $\alpha$ is less than 1, $\sigma_f$ (the s.d. of deviations around the trend in food prices) will be less than $\sigma_w$ (the s.d. of deviations around the trend in wheat prices), even if the correlation between wheat and food prices is perfect ($r_{rw} = 1$). As it turns out, the estimated value of $\alpha$ is 0.346 (and $\overline{R}^2$ is 0.61) over the years 1540–1738 so that use of wheat prices, and their conversion within the context of King's law into a measure of supply, greatly exaggerates the variability of the food supply during the early modern era (see the appendix to this chapter).

If the deviations around trend in the food supply ($\sigma_{fq}$) are to be estimated from the deviations in wheat prices, what we need to know is the elasticity of the food supply with respect to wheat prices ($\varepsilon_{fw}$) rather than King's law, which, even when properly interpreted, gives only the elasticity of the quantity of wheat demanded with respect to wheat price. Unfortunately, the time series needed to estimate $\sigma_{fq}$ (the s.d. of deviations in the annual quantity of the food supply) for England is not yet available even for recent times, but it is possible to estimate $\sigma_{gq}$ (the s.d. of deviations from trend in an index of all grain yields) after 1884. With this change, the desired elasticity $\varepsilon_{fw}$ can be estimated from Equation (6):

$$\varepsilon_{fw} = \frac{\sigma_{gq}}{\sigma_w} r_{gq,w}, \tag{6}$$

where $\sigma_w$ is the s.d. of proportional deviations from trend on wheat prices. If we assume $r_{gq,w} = 1$, only $\sigma_{gq}$ needs to be estimated because, as indicated earlier, $\sigma_w = 0.220$. When $\sigma_{gq}$ is estimated from data over the period 1884–1913, it turns out to be 0.0300, which puts $\varepsilon_{fw}$ at 0.136.

This provisional estimate of $\varepsilon_{fw}$ implies that even the largest deviation of wheat prices above trend in Hoskins' entire 280-year period (or Wrigley and Schofield's 331-year period) involved a manageable shortfall in the supply of food. Although carry-over stocks were diminished, more than two-thirds of the normal amount – more than a three-month supply – remained over and above all claims for feed, seed, and human consumption.

## FAMINES AMID SURPLUSES: A SUGGESTED MECHANISM

There does not, then, appear to have been a single year after circa 1500 in which the aggregate supply of food was too low to avoid a subsistence crisis. These crises were man-made rather than natural disasters and clearly were avoidable with the technology of the age, as Davenant (1699) and other contemporary men of affairs have pointed out. Famines amid surpluses remain a phenomenon even today, as Amartya Sen (1981) emphasized, not only because foods on a worldwide scale are ample enough to prevent famines but because famines have broken out in certain underdeveloped nations despite good harvests. These famines were caused not by natural disasters but by dramatic redistributions of entitlements to grain. The events that promoted the redistributions of entitlements were sharp rises in the price of grain relative to wages or other types of income received by the lower classes. In the "great Bengal famine" (Flinn 1974; Post 1976; Appleby 1979; Hufton 1983; Tilly 1983) of 1943, for example, the exchange rate between wages and foodgrains declined by 86 percent, despite an "exceptionally high" supply of grain. In this case, the rise in grain prices had nothing to do with the bountifulness of the harvest but was driven by forces outside the agricultural sector. The Bengal famine, Sen points out, was a "boom famine," caused by "powerful inflationary pressures" unleashed by a rapid expansion of public expenditures.

The relevance of the entitlement approach to the interpretation of the social and economic history of the early modem era does not depend on the source of the rise in grain prices that triggers the redistribution of entitlements. It is the similarity in the structural characteristics of traditional societies of the past and of low-income countries today that makes the entitlement approach pertinent (Flinn 1974; Post 1976; Appleby 1979; Hufton 1983; Tilly 1983). At the root of these structural similarities is the highly unequal distribution of wealth and the overarching importance of land as a source of wealth. These twin characteristics lead directly to two other structural features: first, they cause the price elasticity of the total demand for grains to be quite low, and second, they drive a large wedge between the grain demand elasticities of the upper and the lower classes, with the elasticity of the lowest classes having a value that may be ten or twenty times as large as the elasticity of the class of great land magnates. It is these large class differences in demand elasticities (caused by social organization), rather than wide year-to-year swings in harvest yields (caused by variations in weather or other natural phenomena), that were the source of the periodic subsistence crises that afflicted late medieval and early modern England and the Continent.

The remainder of this section sets forth a mechanism that may have produced a world with famines amid surpluses that were more than adequate to have prevented the famines. I have endeavored to make the following model conform as closely as possible to the known facts of English society during the early modem era. The appendix describes my procedures for estimating the key parameters and the sources for these estimates. It also gives the derivations of Equations (7)–(11).

Equation (7) is a convenient starting point for the estimation of the relevant elasticities:

$$\varepsilon_i = [\theta(1 - \varepsilon_t) - \beta_i]\Psi_i - \bar{\varepsilon}_i \tag{7}$$

where

$\varepsilon_i$ = price elasticity of the demand for grain

$\Psi_i$ = income elasticity of the demand for grain

$\bar{\varepsilon}_i$ = income-adjusted price elasticity of the demand for grain

$\beta_i$ = share of grain in total consumption expenditures

$\theta_i$ = share of income arising from the ownership of grain

$\varepsilon_t$ = price elasticity of the total aggregate demand for grain (see Equation (10))

$i$ = subscript designating the $i$th class

Equation (7) states that the price elasticity of demand for grains of a given class depends not only on $\bar{\varepsilon}_i$ (the income-adjusted price elasticity, which is often referred to as the *substitution elasticity*) but also on the relative magnitude of $(1 - \varepsilon_t)\theta$ (which is the elasticity of nominal income with respect to the price of grain) and $\beta_i$. It follows from (7) that wealthy landlords would have a much more inelastic demand for grain (because the share of their income arising from the ownership of grain-producing lands equaled or exceeded the share of their income that was spent on the consumption of grains, i.e., because $(1 - \varepsilon_t)\theta_i \geq \beta_i$ ) than landless laborers (for whom $\theta_i = 0$ and $\beta_i$ is large).

Table 3.5 divides the English population at the middle of the Wrigley–Schofield period (c. 1700) into four categories or classes, which correspond roughly to the aristocracy and gentry, the yeomanry, artisans and petty shopkeepers, and common laborers (including the unemployed). Out-servants working in the households of the upper classes are included with these classes because their masters provided the food they consumed. In other words, the population embraced by the landlords (class 1 in the table) includes not only the landlords and their immediate families but all of their retainers, high and low. The category titled "farmers and lesser landlords" includes such other owners of food inventories as bakers, brewers, innkeepers, and grain merchants. The two categories are thus defined so that virtually all inventories are owned by the two top classes and virtually none by the two bottom ones.

Table 3.5 also presents my estimates for the share of the English population represented by each of the classes, the normal share of each class in the annual consumption of grain $(\varphi_i\varphi_i)$ and of $\theta_i(1 - \varepsilon_t)$, $\beta_i$, $\Psi_i$, and $\varepsilon_i$ (see the appendix for sources and procedures). The values of $\varphi_i$ shown in column 2 imply that landlords consumed nearly two-thirds more, and yeomen about one-sixth more, grain per capita than the national average (much of it as ale and spirits); that shopkeepers and craftsmen consumed the national average; and that common laborers and paupers consumed about three-quarters of the national average. These values of $\varphi_i$ imply that the average caloric intake of the poor was at about the mean level of Ghana or Chad today (World Bank 1984), whereas that of the landlords was at about the level of U.S. farmers circa 1850 (Fogel and Engerman 1974).

One important implication of Table 3.5 is that although laborers comprised about 44 percent of the population, they accounted for only 33 percent of the normal consumption of foodgrains. Another implication of the table is that the effect of a rise in grain prices on elasticities was quite different for different classes (see columns 6 and 7). In the case of landlords and farmers (classes 1 and 2), the rise in prices had two effects: as owners of surpluses, the rise in prices

TABLE 3.5. *Estimates of Normal Shares in Foodgrain Consumption of the Normal Price Elasticities of the Demand for Foodgrains, by Socioeconomic Class in England c. 1700*

| Class of Household Head | Share in Population | Normal Share in Consumption of the Foodgrains $\varphi_i$ | Share of Grain in Total Expenditure of a Class $\beta_i$ | Elasticity of Nominal Income with Respect to the Price of Grain $\theta_i(1 - \varepsilon_i)$ | Income Elasticity $\psi_i$ | Income-Adjusted Price Elasticity $\bar{\varepsilon}_i$ | Price Elasticity $\varepsilon_i$ |
|---|---|---|---|---|---|---|---|
| Landlords (incl. servants and retainers) | 0.11 | 0.18 | 0.15 | 0.23 | 0.10 | 0.02 | 0.01 |
| Farmers and lesser landlords (incl. servants) | 0.34 | 0.39 | 0.15 | 0.35 | 0.19 | 0.05 | 0.01 |
| Shopkeepers, minor professionals, and craftsmen (incl. servants) | 0.11 | 0.11 | 0.35 | 0.00 | 0.36 | 0.19 | 0.32 |
| Laborers and the unemployed (not incl. servants covered in preceding lines) | 0.44 | 0.33 | 0.70 | 0.00 | 0.92 | 0.41 | 1.05 |

increased their income, while as consumers, it reduced their income. Since the producer's effect is stronger than the consumer's effect, the income component of the price elasticity (i.e., $[(1 - \varepsilon_t)\theta - \beta]\Psi$) is negative and so offsets the income-adjusted elasticity ($\bar{\varepsilon}$), making the price elasticities of these two classes quite close to zero. In the case of laborers, however, only the consumption effect operated. In this case, the income component of the price elasticity augments $\bar{\varepsilon}$. Although $\bar{\varepsilon}$ is already relatively high, the total price elasticity ($\varepsilon$) is more than twice as high.

The values set forth in Table 3.5 make it possible to estimate the aggregate elasticity of the foodgrain demand for grains ($\varepsilon_c$) by making use of the following relationship:

$$\varepsilon_c = \varphi_1\varepsilon_1 + \varphi_2\varepsilon_2 + \varphi_3\varepsilon_3 + \varphi_4\varepsilon_4. \tag{8}$$

Substituting the appropriate values of $\varphi i$ and $\varepsilon_i$ into (8) yields

$$\varepsilon_c = (0.18)(0.01) + (0.39)(0.01) + (0.11)(0.32)$$
$$+ (0.33)(1.05) = 0.3787. \tag{9}$$

Thus the estimates of class elasticities in Table 3.5 imply that the elasticity of the aggregate foodgrain demand was below 0.5, even though common laborers and paupers, who accounted for nearly half the population, had an elasticity in excess of 1. However, as (8) indicates, it is shares in consumption rather than in population that determine the value of $\varepsilon_c$ : if it were the population shares that mattered, $\varepsilon_c$ would be nearly 30 percent larger than the indicated size.

Although $\varepsilon_c$ is the price elasticity of the aggregate foodgrain demand, it is not the price elasticity of aggregate demand for all grain, which is given by

$$\varepsilon_t = \delta\varepsilon_s + (1 - \delta)\varepsilon_c, \tag{10}$$

where

$\varepsilon_s$ = the price elasticity of demand for grains used as seed, feed, and carry-over inventories

$\delta$ = the share of the total supply used as seed, feed, and carryover inventories

Since about 55 percent of the supply of grains was reserved for carry-over, seed, and feed, the estimation of $\varepsilon_s$ is critical. If $\varepsilon_s$ were 0, $\varepsilon_t$ would be only 0.174. There is much commentary in the literature that suggests that that was the case.[11] There was, for example, virtually no long-term variation in the amount of wheat seed planted per acre, which appears to have stood at about 2.5 bushels from the fourteenth century to the nineteenth (Hoskins 1968; Wrigley 1987). During the Irish famine, it was noted that many farmers starved to death while holding on to the stocks of potatoes and grains they had set aside to pay their rents (Flinn 1981). Farmers also were apparently loath to dip into grain set aside for animal feed.[12] It is not possible with the data currently at hand to estimate $\varepsilon_s$ directly, but it is possible to estimate $\varepsilon_t$ and then to solve (10) for $\varepsilon_s$. Using the estimate of $\sigma_{gp}$ (the s.d. of deviations in grain prices around trend) for the period 1540–1738, and of $\sigma_{gp}$ for 1884–1913, $\varepsilon_t$ can be estimated from

$$\varepsilon_t = \frac{\sigma_{gq}}{\sigma_{gp}} r_{gq.gp}, \tag{11}$$

again assuming $r_{gq.gp} = 1$. The resulting value of $\varepsilon_t$ is 0.178, which tends to confirm the belief that during the early modern era, the elasticity of the demand for stocks held in reserve to ensure feed, seed, rental payments, and other contingencies was close to 0.[13]

---

[11] The suggestion that $\varepsilon_s$ is close to 0 may appear to conflict with the preceding discussion, which indicated that carry-over inventories were more than adequate to feed the destitute without impinging on seed reserves. However, the fact that carry-over inventories were adequate to feed the destitute does not mean that the owners of the inventories were willing to release them at prevailing prices, let alone at normal prices.

[12] We do not yet know what made the feed demand for grain so inelastic. However, it may be that feedgrains were used primarily for work animals and that farmers believed that skimping on feedgrains would weaken the horses and oxen on whose well-being the following year's crop would depend.

[13] See the appendix for the sources and procedures in estimating $\sigma_{gq}$ and $\sigma_{gp}$. In Fogel (1986b), I argued that $\varepsilon_s$ was only moderately inelastic, despite the fact that English agricultural historians have implicitly or explicitly maintained that the seed and feed elasticities of demand were quite low (Hoskins 1964, 1968; Everitt 1967). The same point was vigorously argued by E. A. Wrigley in an exchange of letters that we had in 1985. However, it was only after I estimated from data on yields for the period 1884–1913 that I reconsidered my earlier judgment and more closely examined the evidence that Wrigley called to my attention. The weight of that evidence supports Wrigley's position.

TABLE 3.6. *The Consequence of Shifting Entitlement Exchange Ratios on the Share of Each Class in the Reduced Crop and on the per Capita Consumption of Each Class*

| | Normal Share (%) of Each Class in Foodgrain Crop $Q_d = Q_i = 1$ $P = 1$ $\varepsilon_i = 0.178$ | Case Where $Q_i = 0.95$ | |
|---|---|---|---|
| | | Share of Each Class in Reduced Output of Foodgrain at Market-Clearing Price (%) | % Decline of Each Class from Normal Per Capita Consumption of Foodgrains |
| Landlords (incl. servants and retainers) | 0.18 | 0.201 | 0.2 |
| Farmers and lesser landlords (incl. servants) | 0.39 | 0.436 | 0.2 |
| Shopkeepers, minor professionals, and craftsmen (incl. servants) | 0.11 | 0.11 | 10.9 |
| Laborers and the unemployed (not incl. servants covered in preceding lines) | 0.33 | 0.252 | 31.9 |

An important implication of the model set forth in this section is that a relatively small decline in the supply of grain could have produced a sharp rise in prices. Because of the highly inelastic demand for inventories, virtually all of the adjustment in entitlements would have taken place among consumers. As Table 3.6 shows, even a shortfall of supply as small as 5 percent triggers significant shifts in the shares of grain consumed by different classes. In the case of landlords, the rise in their share largely offsets the decline in output so that their per capita consumption is virtually unchanged. In the case of laborers, however, the decline in their share reinforces the decline in output so that their per capita consumption is down by 32 percent. It is worth noting that although output declines by 5 percent, aggregate foodgrain consumption declines by 11 percent. Because the demand for grain reserves for feed, seed, and rentals is so inelastic, virtually the entire shortfall is borne by foodgrain consumption.

The sharp decline in consumption of the laboring class (when $Q_s = 0.95$) is due to the combination of its high elasticity of demand ($\varepsilon_4 = 1.05$) and the sharp rise in price ($P$ goes to 1.44). It should be noted that about a quarter of the indicated price rise is due not directly to a decline in $Q_s$ from 1 to 0.95 but to the decline in the value of $\varepsilon_t$ as the price increases. If $\varepsilon_t$ had remained constant, the decline in $Q_s$ would have led to a 33 percent increase in prices instead of a 44 percent increase. In other words, one of the effects of the shifting distribution of entitlements is to reduce $\varepsilon_t$, both because $\varepsilon_c$ declines and because $\delta$ increases. It follows that an initial rise in prices tends to feed on itself, even in the absence of speculative hoarding, by increasing the share of grain entitlements held by classes with a highly inelastic demand.

### THE LONG STRUGGLE TO REPAIR THE SYSTEM OF FOOD DISTRIBUTION

Reductions in the national supply of grain by as much as 5 percent were rare events during the early modern era, occurring about once a century. However, deficits of 4 percent in the grain supply were more frequent, occurring about once a generation. When such events occurred, their impact was devastating on laborers and the unemployed, among whom the subsistence crisis was largely confined. Such great events, which reduced a normally poor diet to starvation levels, were social disasters. Whatever their impact on mortality, they could not be ignored by either local or national authorities.

Nor were they. In England during the Tudor and Stuart eras, containing the damage caused by grain shortages was a primary objective of the state. Famines were viewed not only as natural and economic disasters but also as political ones (Everitt 1967). The basic strategy of the Crown was to leave the grain market to its own devices during times of plenty, except to guard against abuses of weights and measures and to foil plots to corner markets. (Even these measures provoked hostility from provincial justices and traders, who resented the attempts of the central government to usurp local rights; as a result of their pressure, the Long Parliament passed legislation that made it impossible for a uniform system of weights and measures to be established up until the nineteenth century; see Everitt 1967.)

In years of grain shortage, however, the state overrode the complaints of traders, merchants, brewers, bakers, and other processors. In 1587 and in subsequent years of dearth, the Privy Council issued a Book of Orders, which instructed local magistrates to determine the grain inventories of all farmers, factors, maltsters, and bakers; to force holders of inventories to supply their grain to artificers and laborers at relatively low prices; to suppress unnecessary taverns and unnecessary expenditures of corn in manufacturing; and to prevent all export abroad and limit transportation at home (Everitt 1967).

It was, of course, easier to issue such orders than to enforce them. Despite the specter of popular upheaval that spurred the authorities, they found it difficult to gain control of inventories or to curb the rise in prices. Despite the attempts of magistrates, corn continued to be exported abroad and sold to brewers. Innkeepers who had contracted for their supplies before the harvest insisted on the enforcement of their contracts. When maltsters complied with suppression orders, they often found themselves prosecuted by customers who had sent barley to them to be malted. Caught in the middle, many tradesmen and processors were driven to poverty by regulations intended to prevent just that. The procedure enraged farmers and tradesmen who were subject to the inquisitional searches of bailiffs and constables, often for no better reason than the testimony of a common informer (Everitt 1967).

Because of the resistance of landlords, farmers, merchants, maltsters, and other owners of stock, it has been argued that government efforts to gain control of grain surpluses and to reduce the volatility of prices were a failure. Some hold that the paternalistic restrictions of the government were actually counterproductive because the effort to uncover hidden stocks of grain served to foster alarm and push prices up. Instead of promoting greater efficiency in the market, these restrictions thwarted the activities of middlemen, whose function was to balance demand and supply by moving grain from places in which it was abundant to those in which it was scarce (Gras 1915; Everitt 1967). Others believe that Tudor–Stuart paternalism actually worked. Although it might have taken a while for the scheme to ration grain on behalf of the poor to become effective, numerous instances can be cited during the reigns of James I and Charles I in which concealed grain was brought to market and sold to the poor at reduced prices (Supple 1964; Everitt 1967; Lipson 1971).

Evidence bearing on this debate can be obtained by relating the variance in deviations of wheat prices from trend to the dominant policies of government in particular periods of time. For this purpose, I have defined four periods. The first is 1541–1599, which represents the years before the paternalistic apparatus for controlling grain supplies during dearth was in place or became effective. Although precedents for the intervention of the Privy Council during a subsistence crisis may be found during the reign of Henry VIII, it was not until the end of the third decade of Elizabeth's reign that a potentially effective system was spelled out. The Book of Orders, published in 1587, listed thirty-three measures aimed at giving the authorities enough control over the supply to permit the sale of grain for consumption directly to laborers at moderate prices. It set forth a mechanism at the local level for enforcing the regulations; assigned specific roles to sheriffs, justices of the peace, and mayors; and called for special juries of the leaders in each community to oversee the search for surplus stocks (Gras 1915; Lipson 1971).

Devising a minute system of regulations and making it work are two separate matters, especially since the local justices, who were the linchpin of the system, were lukewarm to the policy. The system did not become effective until the Privy Council provided the zeal and the administrative pressure required to mobilize local authorities. The turning point came in 1597, with the passage of a series of new laws aimed at alleviating poverty, laws framed in response to three years of turbulence set off by a combination of a depression and severe dearth. Fearing spontaneous insurrections, the Privy Council not only promoted the new legislation but sought to enforce vigorously its Book of Orders.

Beginning about 1600, the Council brought increasingly heavy pressure to bear on the local authorities. Proclamations were much the same as they had been, but the orders were more detailed and the follow-up more systematic. Local authorities responded. In some cities and towns, public granaries were established so that stores would be available to sell grain to the poor below market price; the making of malt was regulated by quotas; and searches for surpluses were more thorough. By 1631, the sale of grain to the poor below market prices had become widespread (Jordan 1959; Supple 1964; Leonard 1965; Lipson 1971).

This paternalistic system began to unravel with the English Civil War. Indeed, the heavy-handed intervention of the Privy Council with local authorities to relieve poverty was one of the grievances of the opposition to Charles I. However, although the victory of Parliament over the King enabled those who sought free markets and the protection of property to have their way, the paternalistic system did not collapse at once. The same inertia at the local level that made it so difficult for Elizabeth and the early Stuarts to effect their reforms now operated in the opposite direction. Although the landholders and merchants who dominated Parliament developed a legislative program aimed at unshackling farmers, producers, and merchants from the restraints that had been imposed on them, local authorities continued to prosecute those who sought to profit from dearth at the expense of the poor. However, as Parliament implemented its new program, local authorities veered in the new direction, and the paternalistic apparatus atrophied (Chartres 1985).

The motivation for the switch in government policy has been debated by historians but not resolved. Some investigators believe that after the English Civil War, landowning classes, unrestrained by the bureaucratic paternalism of the Tudors and the early Stuarts, lifted restrictions on producers and merchants and placed a tariff on imports as acts of self-aggrandizement. That process was, in this view, abetted by a grateful William III, who supported export bounties on grain as one of his favors to the class that put him in power (Barnes 1930; Rose 1961; Lipson 1971). Others, noting that the principal economic problem after the Restoration was economic stagnation and unemployment, believe that new measures were aimed at stimulating a depressed agriculture, promoting the reclamation of the fens and other wastelands, improving the system of marketing and transportation, and promoting industry. According to this view, it was not so much the landlords but the ordinary tenant farmers who would have been impoverished by outworn policies that continued to drive prices down. In the face of an agricultural depression that gripped not only England but the Continent as well, the key issue was the encouragement of agricultural diversification and the industrial production of agricultural products,

TABLE 3.7. *Analysis of the Variance in the Deviations of Wheat Prices from Trend during Four Periods between 1541 and 1745, England*

| Period | Dates | $S^2$ (Measured as % Deviations from Trend) |
|---|---|---|
| The years preceding paternalist regulation or during which the machinery for regulation was being put in place | 1541–1599 | 935 |
| The apogee of regulation | 1600–1640 | 270 |
| The dismantling of the regulatory machinery | 1641–1699 | 625 |
| The dominance of government policies aimed at promoting agricultural growth and diversification by raising prices and developing markets | 1700–1745 | 633 |

*Source:* Wheat prices are from Hoskins (1964, 1968).

including beer and spirits (Everitt 1967; Lipson 1971; Abel 1980; Chartres 1985; Thirsk 1985).

Whatever the motivation for the switch in policy, it was the abandonment of the Tudor–Stuart program of food relief, and not natural disasters or the technological backwardness of agriculture, that subjected England to periodic famines for two centuries further. That conclusion is implied by Table 3.7, which shows that during the period 1600–1640, when government relief efforts were at their apogee, the variance of wheat prices around trend declined to less than one-third of the level of the preceding era. That large a drop cannot be explained plausibly by chance variations in weather because the $F$ value is statistically significant at the 0.0001 level.[14] Nor is it likely that the sharp rise in the variance of wheat prices during the last six decades of the seventeenth century was the result of chance variations in weather.[15]

[14] The result of the $F$ test would not have changed if Equation (11) had been used to obtain the implied values of $\sigma_{gq}$ (assuming $\varepsilon_t = 0.178$) because $(0.178)^2$ would appear in both the numerator and denominator of the $F$ statistic and hence would cancel out.

[15] The relevant $F$ values are significant at the 0.004 level.

In the absence of government action to reduce prices during grain shortages, workers took to the streets, and price-fixing riots became a standard feature of the eighteenth century. During the early decades of the eighteenth century, the government sought to cope with such outbreaks by enforcing vagrancy and settlement laws and by force (Rose 1961; Lipson 1971). During the late 1750s, however, after food riots of unprecedented scope and intensity, proposals for the government to intervene vigorously in the grain market (to return to the Tudor–Stuart policies), including proposals to reestablish public granaries, reemerged. As the battle over these questions ebbed and flowed during the next half century, the government, at both local and national levels, gradually shifted toward more vigorous intervention in the grain market. However, it was not until the nineteenth century that government control over stocks became adequate to reduce the variance in wheat prices to the level that prevailed at the apogee of Tudor–Stuart paternalism. By the middle of the nineteenth century, famines had been conquered, not because the weather had shifted, or because of improvements in technology, but because government policy (at least with respect to its own people)[16] had unalterably shifted back to the ideas and practices of commonweal that had prevailed during 1600–1640 (Barnes 1930; Post 1977).[17]

## CHRONIC MALNUTRITION AND THE SECULAR DECLINE IN MORTALITY

Had the political will been present, a system of public relief adequate to deal with grain crises could have been in place long before the nineteenth century. So much of the famine-related mortality, and much related suffering short of death between 1640 and 1815, could have been avoided. However, as Table 3.1 shows, even complete success in

---

[16] The Irish famine makes this qualification necessary. As Mokyr (1985) has emphasized, if Ireland had been considered an integral part of the British community, the British government might have felt compelled to intervene much more vigorously than it actually did.

[17] In this connection, it is worth noting that famines came to an end early in the nineteenth century not only in England, where per capita consumption of calories appears to have reached levels by 18-IV that are comparable to modem-day India, but also in countries such as France, where average caloric consumption was 15%–20% lower. This issue is discussed more fully in the next section.

the struggle to eliminate famines would have left the level of mortality in normal times shockingly high. Indeed, that table undoubtedly exaggerates the extent of famine mortality because the available evidence suggests that in the English case, less than 10 percent of all crisis mortality between 1541 and 1871 was due to famines (Fogel 1986b).

Although the possibility that famines might have had only a small impact on aggregate mortality had been anticipated (Le Brun 1971; Flinn 1974, 1981). Wrigley and Schofield provided the data needed to measure the national impact. By demonstrating that famines and famine mortality are a secondary issue in the escape from the high-aggregate mortality of the early modern era, they have indirectly pushed to the top of research agendas the issue of chronic malnutrition and its relationship to the secular decline in mortality. It is clear that the new questions cannot be addressed by relating annual deviations of mortality (around trend) to annual deviations of supplies of food (from their trend). What is now at issue is how the trend in malnutrition might be related to the trend in mortality and how to identify the factors that determined each of these secular trends.

The new problems require new data and new analytical procedures. In this connection, one must come to grips with the thorny issue of the distinction between diet (which represents gross nutrition) and malnutrition (which represents net nutrition: the nutrients available to sustain physical development). I will not dwell on this distinction here (which is set forth in Floud 1992) but will only emphasize that when I mean *gross nutrition*, I will use the term *diet*, and that such other terms as *malnutrition, undernutrition, net nutrition*, and *nutritional status* are meant to designate the balance between the nutrient intake (diet) and the claims on that intake.

Malnutrition can be caused either by an inadequate diet or by claims on that diet (including work and disease) so great as to produce widespread malnutrition despite a nutrient intake that in other circumstances might be deemed adequate. There can be little doubt that the high disease rates prevalent during the early modern era would have caused malnutrition even with extraordinary diets, that is, diets high in calories, proteins, and most other critical nutrients. I believe that the United States during 1820–1880 is a case in point (see Fogel 1986b, 1991). However, recent research indicates that for many European nations before the middle of the nineteenth century, the national production of food was at such low levels that the lower classes were bound to have been malnourished under any conceivable circumstance and that the high disease rates of the period were not merely a cause of malnutrition but undoubtedly, to a considerable degree, a consequence of exceedingly poor diets.

Recently developed biomedical techniques, when integrated with several standard economic techniques, make it possible to probe deeply into the extent and the demographic consequences of chronic malnutrition during the eighteenth and nineteenth centuries. The biomedical techniques include improved approaches to the estimation of survival levels of caloric consumption and of the caloric requirements of various types of labor; epidemiological studies of the connection between stature and the risk of both mortality and chronic diseases; and epidemiological studies of the connection between body mass indexes (BMIs) and the risk of mortality. The economic techniques include various methods of characterizing size distributions of income and calories as well as methods of relating measures of nutrition to measures of income and productivity.

## Energy Cost Accounting: The Case of Britain and France during the Last Quarter of the Eighteenth Century

Historical estimates of mean caloric consumption per capita have been derived from several sources, including national food balance sheets and household consumption surveys. The various problems attendant on using these sources have been described elsewhere (see Fogel 1987). Despite their limitations, Toutain's (1971) time series of food consumption in France and the household surveys of English food consumption toward the end of the eighteenth century (Shammas 1984) indicate that in each of these countries, a majority of the population was malnourished (Fogel 1987).

Toutain (1971), on the basis of a national food balance sheet, has estimated that the per capita consumption of calories in France was 1,753 during 1781–1790 and 1,846 during 1803–1812. Converted into calories per consuming unit (equivalent adult male), the figures become about 2,290 and 2,410 calories, respectively. Data in the household budget studies recently reexamined by economic historians indicate that English daily consumption during 1785–1795 averaged about 2,700 calories per consuming unit (Shammas 1984; Fogel 1987).

One way of assessing these two estimates is by considering their distributional implications. As noted elsewhere, all of the known distributions of the average daily consumption of calories for populations are not only reasonably well described by the lognormal distribution but also have coefficients of variation that lie between 0.2 and 0.4 – a narrow range, which is determined at the top end by the human capacity to use energy and the distribution of body builds and at the bottom end by the requirement for basal metabolism and the prevailing death rate (Fogel 1987). Consideration of available evidence on mortality rates (Bourgeois-Pichat 1965; Weir 1984) and the findings of Goubert (1960, 1973), Bernard ([1969] 1975), Hufton (1974), Kaplan (1976), and others on the condition of the lower classes in France during the late ancient regime rule out either 0.2 or 0.4 as plausible estimates of the coefficient of variation and suggest that 0.3 is the best approximation in the light of current knowledge.[18]

Table 3.8 displays the caloric distribution for England and France implied by the available evidence. Several points about these distributions, which lend support to Toutain's estimate for the French and the estimates derived for the English from the budget studies, are worth noting. First, the average levels are not out of keeping with recent experiences in the less developed nations. Low as it is, Toutain's estimate of the French supply of calories is above the average supply of calories in 1965 estimated for such nations as Pakistan, Rwanda, and Algeria and only slightly less (by thirty-nine calories) than that of Indonesia. The English estimate is above that for thirty less developed nations in 1965, including China, Bolivia, the Philippines, and Honduras, and only slightly (by thirty-seven calories) below India (World Bank 1987).

Second, the distributional implications of the two estimates are consistent with both qualitative and quantitative descriptions of the diets of various social classes (Drummond and Wilbraham 1958; Pullar 1970; Rose 1971; Tilly 1971; Goubert 1973; Wilson 1973; Hufton 1974; Tilly 1975; Blum 1978; Burnett 1979; Frijhoff and Julia 1979;

---

[18] The main conclusions summarized in this section are robust to any value of the coefficient of variation in the range $0.3 \pm 0.1$.

TABLE 3.8. A Comparison of the Probable French and English
Distributions of the Daily Consumption of kcal per Consuming Unit
toward the End of the Eighteenth Century

| | France c. 1785 | | England c. 1790 | |
| | $\overline{X} = 2290$ $(S/X) = 0.3$ Daily kcal | | $\overline{X} = 2790$ $(S/X) = 0.3$ Daily kcal | |
| Decile | Consumption | Cumulative % | Consumption | Cumulative % |
| --- | --- | --- | --- | --- |
| (1) Highest | 3,672 | 100 | 4,329 | 100 |
| (2) Ninth | 2,981 | 84 | 3,514 | 84 |
| (3) Eighth | 2,676 | 71 | 3,155 | 71 |
| (4) Seventh | 2,457 | 59 | 2,897 | 59 |
| (5) Sixth | 2,276 | 48 | 2,684 | 48 |
| (6) Fifth | 2,114 | 38 | 2,492 | 38 |
| (7) Fourth | 1,958 | 29 | 2,309 | 29 |
| (8) Third | 1,798 | 21 | 2,120 | 21 |
| (9) Second | 1,614 | 12 | 1,903 | 13 |
| (10) First | 1,310 | 6 | 1,545 | 6 |

Source and procedures: See Fogel (1987, esp. tables 4 and 5 and n.6).

Hufton 1983; Cole and Postgate [1938] 1976). For example, Bernard's study (Bernard [1969] 1975) of marriage contracts made in the Gevaudan during the third quarter of the eighteenth century revealed that the average ration provided for parents in complete pensions contained about 1,674 calories. Since the average age of a male parent at the marriage of his first surviving child was about fifty-nine, the preceding figure implies a diet of about 2,146 calories per consuming unit (Fogel 1987). That figure falls at the forty-seventh percentile of the estimated French distribution (Table 3.8, distribution A), which is quite consistent with the class of peasants described by Bernard.

The two estimates are also consistent with the death rates of each nation. The crude death rate in France circa 1790 was about 36.1 per 1,000, while the figure for England circa 1790 was about 26.7 per 1,000 (Wrigley and Schofield 1981; Weir 1984). It is plausible that much of the difference was due to the larger proportion of French than English who were literally starving (Scrimshaw 1987). The French distribution of calories implies that 2.48 percent of the population had caloric consumption below basal metabolism (the minimum energy required for the functioning of the body).[19] Table 3.8 implies that the proportion of the English below basal metabolism was 0.66 percent. If a quarter of these starving individuals died each year (see Fogel 1987), they would account for about one-fifth (6.6 per 1,000) of the French crude death rate but only about one-sixteenth of the English rate (1.7 per 1,000) and for about half of the gap between the crude death rates of the two nations.[20]

What, then, are the principal provisional findings about caloric consumption at the end of the eighteenth century in France and England? One is the exceedingly low level of food production, especially in France, at the start of the Industrial Revolution. Another is the exceedingly low level of work capacity permitted by the food supply, even after allowing for the reduced requirements for maintenance because of small stature and reduced body mass (cf. Freudenberger and Cummings 1976). In France, the bottom 10 percent of the labor force lacked the energy for regular work, and the next 10 percent had enough energy for less than 3 hours of light work daily (0.52 hours of heavy work). Although the English situation was somewhat better, the bottom 3 percent of its labor force lacked the energy for any work, but the balance of the bottom 20 percent had enough energy for about 6 hours of light work (1.09 hours of heavy work) each day.[21]

That the English ultrapoor were better off than the French ultrapoor was due partly to the greater productivity of English agriculture (as measured by the per capita production of calories). However, the distribution of income was so unequal in England that, had it not been for the English system of poor relief, the proportion of the

[19] For a discussion of the concept of basal metabolism and other components of energy requirement, see FAO/WHO/UNU (1985), Payne (1992), Srinivasan (1992), and Osmani (1992).

[20] This discussion takes account of the incidence of mortality only among those in each country whose consumption of calories was below basal metabolism. However, there were many other individuals who were at increased risk of death because they were malnourished, even though the degree of malnourishment was less extreme; cf. the discussion of Table 3.8.

[21] Even small amounts of common agricultural or urban manual labor would have put such malnourished individuals on a path toward consuming their own tissue and, if continued long enough, would have, sooner or later, resulted in death. These are the people who constitute Marx's "lumpenproletariat," Mayhew's "street folk," Huxley's "substrata," King's "unproductive classes" consuming more than they produced, and the French *gens de néant* (Himmelfarb 1983; Laslett 1984).

English who starved would have been nearly as great as that of the French. In response to the bread riots of the eighteenth century, English authorities substantially expanded the system of poor relief. Between 1750 and 1801, poor relief increased at a real rate of 2.3 percent per annum, which was nearly three times as fast as the growth of either gross national product or the pauper class (Mitchell and Deane 1962; Marshall 1968; Rose 1971; Crafts 1985). Consequently, by circa 1790, relief payments to the ultrapoor had become substantial, more than doubling the income of households in the lowest decile of the English income distribution. In pre-Revolutionary France, on the other hand, the average annual relief provided to the ultrapoor could purchase daily only about one ounce of bread per person (Fogel 1987). The responsiveness of the British government to the bread riots of the poor (Barnes 1930; Rose 1961; Marshall 1968) not only kept the English death rate from soaring but may have spared Britain from a revolution of the French type.

### The Implications of Stature and Body Mass Indexes for the Explanation of Secular Trends in Morbidity and Mortality

The available anthropometric data tend to confirm the basic results of the analysis based on energy cost accounting: chronic malnutrition was widespread in Europe during the eighteenth and nineteenth centuries. Furthermore, such malnutrition seems to have been responsible for much of the very high mortality rates during this period. Moreover, nearly 11 percent of the decline in mortality rates between 1750 and 1875 appears to be explained by the marked improvement in anthropometric measures of malnutrition. This section summarizes evidence bearing on the relationship between mortality and two anthropometric measures – height at maturity and BMI – that are discussed in more detail elsewhere (Fogel 1986a, 1987, 1991, 1993; Fogel and Floud 1991; Fogel et al. 1992).

Height and body mass indexes measure different aspects of malnutrition and health. Height is a net rather than a gross measure of nutrition. Moreover, although changes in height during the growing years are sensitive to current levels of nutrition, mean final height reflects the accumulated past nutritional experience of individuals over all of their growing years, including the fetal period. Thus it follows that when

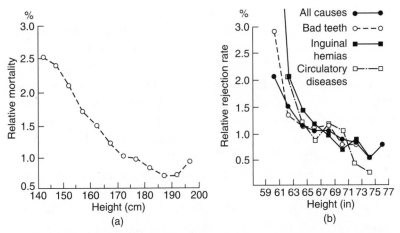

FIGURE 3.1. A comparison of the relationship between body height and relative risk in two populations: (a) relative mortality rates among Norwegian men aged forty to fifty-nine, 1963–1979; (b) relative rejection rates for chronic conditions in a sample of 4,245 men aged twenty-three to forty-nine examined for the U.S. Union Army. *Sources:* Waaler (1984); Fogel et al. (1986).

final heights are used to explain differences in adult mortality rates, they reveal the effect not of adult levels of nutrition on adult mortality rates but of nutritional levels during infancy, childhood, and adolescence on adult mortality rates. A weight-for-height index, conversely, reflects primarily the current nutritional status.

A number of recent studies have established the predictive power of height and BMI with respect to morbidity and monality.[22] The results of two of these studies are summarized in Figures 3.1 and 3.2. Figure 3.1a reproduces a diagram by Waaler (1984). It shows that short Norwegian men aged forty to fifty-nine at risk between 1963 and 1979 were much more likely to die than tall men. Indeed,

---

[22] Many of the issues and some of the evidence regarding the relationship between anthropometric measures, nutritional status, and risk of death are discussed in this volume by Gopalan (1992), Payne (1992), Srinivasan (1992), and Osmani (1992). Most of the literature linking anthropometric measures to morbidity and mortality rates focuses on children aged five or younger. The literature relating stature and weight to mortality rates at adult ages is more limited. The best study to date is for Norway, reported in Waaler (1984). See Fogel (1986a; 1987), Fogel et al. (1986), Fogel (1987), and Fogel and Floud (1991) for a discussion of these matters for the United States and several European countries between 1750 and 1975; see Floud et al. (1990) on Britain and Komlos (1987) on Austria and Hungary.

the risk of mortality for men with heights of 165 cm (65.0 inches) was on average 71 percent greater than that of men who measured 182.5 cm (71.9 inches). Figure 3.1b shows that height was also an important predictor of the relative likelihood that men aged twenty-three to forty-nine would be rejected from the U.S. Union Army during 1861–1865 because of chronic diseases. Despite significant differences in mean heights, ethnicities, environmental circumstances, the array and severity of diseases, and time, the patterns of height and relative risk are strikingly similar. Both the Norwegian curve and the U.S. all-causes curve have relative risks that reach a minimum of between 0.6 and 0.7 at a height of about 187.5 cm. Both reach a relative risk of about 2 at about 152.5 cm. The similarity of the two risk curves in Figure 3.1, despite the differences in conditions and attendant circumstances, suggests that the relative risk of morbidity and mortality depends on the deviation of height not from the *current* mean but from an *ideal* mean: the mean associated with full genetic potential.[23]

Waaler (1984) has also studied the relationship in Norway between BMIs and the risk of death in a sample of 1.7 million individuals. Curves summarizing his findings are shown in Figure 3.2 for both men and women. Although the observed values of the BMI ($kg/m^2$) ranged between 17 and 39, over 80 percent of the males over age forty had BMIs within the range 21–29. Within the range 22–28, the curve is relatively flat, with the relative risk of mortality hovering close to 1.0. However, at BMIs of less than 22 and over 28, the risk of death rises quite sharply as the BMI moves away from its mean value. It will be noticed that the BMI curves are much more symmetrical than the height curves in Figure 3.1, which indicates that high BMIs are as risky as low ones.

Although Figures 3.1 and 3.2 are revealing, neither one singly nor both together are sufficient to shed light on the debate over whether moderate stunting impairs health when weight-for-height is adequate because Figure 3.1 is not controlled for weight and Figure 3.2 is

---

[23] For a further discussion of this possibility, see Fogel (1987) and Fogel and Floud (1991). It is important to keep in mind that the denominators of the relative risk curves in both parts of Figure 3.1 are the average mortality or morbidity rate computed over all heights. Consequently, the curves shown here will not necessarily shift merely because of a change in the overall crude death rate or the corresponding morbidity rate.

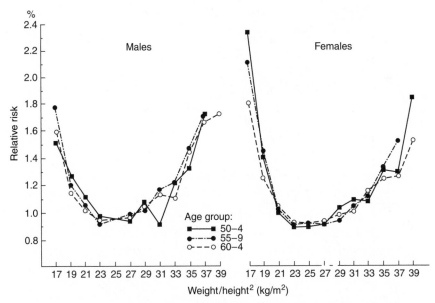

FIGURE 3.2. The relationship between BMI and prospective risk among Norwegian adults aged fifty to sixty-four at risk, 1963–1979. *Source:* Waaler (1984).

only partially controlled for height (Fogel 1987; Fogel and Floud 1991). To get at the small-but-healthy issue, one needs an isomortality surface that relates the risk of death to both height and weight simultaneously.[24] Such a surface, presented in Figure 3.3, was fitted to Waaler's data by a procedure described elsewhere (Fogel 1991). Transecting the isomortality map are lines that give the locus of BMI between 16 and 34 and a curve giving the weights that minimize risk at each height.

Figure 3.3 shows that even when body weight is maintained at what Figure 3.2 indicates is an ideal level (BMI = 21), short men are at substantially greater risk of death than tall men. Thus an adult male with a BMI of 25 who is 162 cm tall is at about 55 percent greater risk of death than a male at 183 cm who also has a BMI of 25. Figure 3.3 also shows that the ideal BMI (the BMI that minimizes the risk of death) varies with height. A BMI of 25 is ideal for men in the

---

[24] See Osmani (1992) for a description of the controversy; also cf. Gopalan (1992) and Payne (1992).

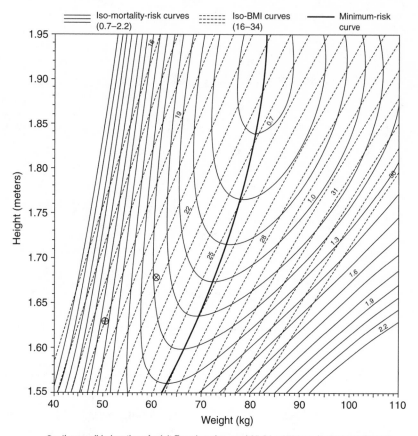

⊕ = the possible location of adult French males aged 25-34 *c*.1790 on the isomortality map. The predicted risk for French males is 1.63.

⊗ = the possible location of comparable English males *c*.1790. The predicted risk for English males is 1.18.

FIGURE 3.3. Isomortality curves of relative risk for height and weight among Norwegian males aged fifty to sixty-four, 1963–1979. *Note:* All risks are measured relative to the average risk of mortality (calculated over all heights and weights) among Norwegian males aged fifty to sixty-four. *Source:* Fogel (1987).

neighborhood of 176 cm, but for tall men (greater than 183 cm), the ideal BMI is between 22 and 24, while for short men (under 164 cm), it is a bit under 26.

Before using Figure 3.3 to evaluate the relationship between chronic malnutrition and the secular decline in mortality rates after 1750, three issues in the interpretation of that figure need to be addressed. First, since an individual's height cannot be varied by changes in nutrition after maturity, adults can move to a more desirable BMI only by changing weight. I therefore interpret the $x$ axis as a measure of the effect of the current nutritional status of mature males on adult mortality rates. Moreover, since most stunting takes place under the age of three (Tanner 1982; Horton 1985; Martorell 1985; Steckel 1995), I interpret the $y$ axis as a measure of the effect of nutritional deprivation in utero or early in childhood on the risk of mortality at middle and late ages (cf. Tanner 1982; Steckel 1983; Fogel et al. 1992).

Second, in applying Figure 3.3 to the evaluation of secular trends in nutrition and mortality, I assume that for Europeans, environmental factors have been decisive in explaining the secular increase in heights, not only for population means but also for individuals in particular families. The reasonableness of this assumption becomes evident when one considers the issue of shortness. If shortness is defined as a given number of standard deviations below a changing mean (i.e., if "short" is two standard deviations below the mean, whether the mean is 164 cm or 183 cm), then genetic and environmental factors may be difficult to disentangle. If, however, shortness is defined in absolute terms, say, as applying to all males with heights below 168 cm, then it is quite clear that most shortness in Europe and America during the eighteenth and much of the nineteenth centuries was determined by environmental rather than genetic factors.

The point at issue can be clarified by considering the experience of the Netherlands. Shortness has virtually disappeared from that country during the past century and a half. Today, less than 2 percent of young adult males are below 168 cm, but circa 1855, about two-thirds were below that height. Because there has been little change in the gene pool of the Dutch during the period, it must have been changes in environmental circumstances, nutrition, and health that eliminated about 95 percent of all short males from the Dutch population (Van Wieringen 1986; Fogel 1987). Given current growth rates in the mean final height of the Netherlands, the remaining men shorter than 168 cm may yet be virtually eliminated from the Dutch population.

The Dutch case illustrates the general secular pattern of physical growth in the nations of Western Europe. The secular increase in mean final heights, which ranged between 10 and 20 cm (4 and 8 inches) over the past two hundred years, cannot be attributed to natural selection or genetic drift because these processes require much longer time spans. Nor can it be attributed to heterosis (hybrid vigor) because the populations in question have remained relatively homogeneous and because the effects of heterosis in human populations have been shown, both empirically and theoretically, to be quite small (Cavalli-Sforza and Bodmer 1971; Van Wieringen 1978; Fogel et al. 1983; Martorell 1985; Mueller 1986). Only the top 6 percent of the Dutch height distribution circa 1855 overlaps with the bottom 6 percent of the current distribution of final heights. Because the Dutch mean is still increasing, and we do not yet know the maximum mean genetically obtainable (often referred to as the genetic potential), it may well be that even the 6 percent overlap between the distribution of final heights in the circa 1855 generation and in the latest generation will be cut in the next few decades, perhaps by as much as half.

Third, even if the Norwegian isomortality surface is applicable to European populations generally, the surface may not have been stable over time. Since height-specific and weight-specific mortality rates are measured relative to the CDR for the population as a whole, short-term shifts in the CDR by themselves will not shift the surface. However, fundamental shifts in environment, including changes in medical technology, may shift the risk surface. One way of ascertaining whether there has been a shift in the risk surface is by determining what part of the decline in mortality rates can be explained merely by movements along the surface (i.e., merely by changes in height and weight on the assumption that the surface has been stable since 1750).

The average final heights of men in several European countries over the period from 1750 to modern times are reported in Table 3.9. It will be seen that during the eighteenth century, these Europeans were severely stunted by modern standards. The French cohort of 18-IV is the most stunted, measuring only 160.5 cm (63.2 inches). The next two shortest cohorts are those of Norway for 18-III and Hungary for 18-IV, which measured 163.9 cm (64.5 inches). Britain and Sweden were the tallest populations between 1775 and 1875, although by the end of the period, Norway nearly matched the leaders.

France was intermediate in its early growth rate, with stature increasing about 0.73 cm per quarter between 18-IV and 19-II. However, the French rate of increase sagged slightly over the next half

TABLE 3.9. *Estimated Average Final Heights of Men Who Reached Maturity between 1759 and 1875 in Six European Populations, by Quarter Centuries*

| Date of Maturity | Britain | Norway | Sweden | France | Denmark | Hungary |
|---|---|---|---|---|---|---|
| 18-III | 165.9 | 163.9 | 168.1 | | | 168.7 |
| 18-IV | 167.9 | | 166.7 | 160.5 | 165.7 | 165.8 |
| 19-I | 168.0 | | 166.7 | 164.0 | 165.4 | 163.9 |
| 19-II | 171.6 | | 168.0 | 166.7 | 166.8 | 164.2 |
| 19-III | 169.3 | 168.6 | 169.5 | 165.2 | 165.3 | |
| 20-III | 175.0 | 178.3 | 177.6 | 172.0 | 176.0 | 170.9 |

*Source:* Fogel (1987, table 7) for all columns except France. France: rows 19-I through 19-III were computed from von Meerton (1989), with 0.9 cm added to allow for additional growth between age twenty and maturity (Gould 1869, 104–105). The entry for 18-IV is derived from a linear extrapolation of von Meerton's data for 1815–1836 back to 1788, with 0.9 cm added for additional growth between age twenty and maturity. The entry in 20-III is from Fogel (1987, table 7).

century and hovered between 165.3 and 166.7 cm until the turn of the twentieth century (Floud 1984). British heights increased more rapidly (1.90 cm per quarter century) and for a longer period than French. The accumulated increase over the first seventy-five years (18-III to 19-II) was 5.7 cm, more than three-fifths of the total increase in British heights between 18-III and the current generation of adults. However, British heights declined slightly with the cohort of 19-III and also remained on a plateau for about half a century (Floud et al. 1990). Swedish heights appear to have declined during the last half of the eighteenth century but then to have risen sharply beginning with the second quarter of the nineteenth century, initiating the marked secular increase in Swedish heights that has continued to the present day.

Indeed, over the last century, the three Scandinavian countries shown in Table 3.9 and the Netherlands (Chamla 1983) have had the most vigorous and sustained increases in stature in the Western world, outpacing Britain and the United States (Fogel 1986b). Hungary's growth pattern differs from that of all the other European nations (Komlos 1987): its cohort of 18-III was taller than that of Sweden, but then Hungarian heights declined sharply for half a century, and despite a turnabout in the nineteenth century, Hungary remains one of the shortest populations in Europe – its mean height today is below the level achieved by the British cohort of 19-II.

Data on BMIs for France and Britain during the late eighteenth and most of the nineteenth centuries are much more patchy than those on stature. Consequently, attempts to compare British and French BMIs during this period are necessarily conjectural. It appears that circa 1790, the average English BMI for males about age thirty was between 21 and 22, which is about 10 percent below current levels. The corresponding figure for French males circa 1790 may have been only about 19, which is about 25 percent below current levels (Fogel and Floud 1991). The conjectural nature of these figures makes the attempt to go from anthropometric data to differential mortality rates more illustrative than substantive. However, Figure 3.3 indicates the apparent location of French and English males of 18-IV on the iso-mortality map generated from Waaler's data. These points imply that the French mortality rate should have been about 40 percent higher than that of the English, which is quite close to the estimated ratio of mortality rates for the two countries.[25] In other words, the available data suggest that in 18-IV, both France and Britain were character-ized by the same mortality risk surface (i.e., the same mortality regi-men), and that differences in their average mortality rates are explained largely by differences in their distributions of height and weight-for-height.

This result raises the question as to how much of the decline in Euro-pean mortality rate since 18-IV can be explained merely by increases in stature and BMIs, that is, merely by movements along an unchanging mortality risk surface. For the three countries for which even patchy data are available – England, France, and Sweden – it appears that nearly all of the decline in mortality between 18-IV and 19-III was due to movements along the Waaler mortality surface, since the esti-mated changes in height and BMI appear to explain between 80 and 100 percent of the decline in mortality during this three-quarters of a century. However, movements along the Waaler surface appear to explain only about 50 to 60 percent of the decline in mortality rates

---

[25] The English CDR for eleven years centered on 1790 is 26.7, and 1.40 times that number is 37.3, which is close to the French CDR derived from Weir's data for the eleven years centered on 1790.

after 1875. After 1875, increases in longevity involved factors other than those that exercise their influence through stature and body mass (Fogel 1987; Fogel and Floud 1991).

CONCLUSIONS

Recent findings in economics and demographic history have shed new light on the European escape from hunger and high mortality since 1750. These advances have been stimulated partly by a better integration of biomedical, economic, and demographic analysis and partly by an enormous expansion of the database to which these techniques can be applied. Since we are still at an early stage of some of these investigations, current findings must be considered provisional and subject to change. The seven principal findings of this chapter are as follows:

1. Crisis mortality accounted for less than 5 percent of total mortality in England before 1800, and the elimination of crisis mortality accounted for just 15 percent of the decline in total mortality between the eighteenth and nineteenth centuries. Consequently, regardless of how large a share of crisis mortality is attributed to famines, famines accounted for only a small share of total mortality before 1800.

2. The use of variations in wheat prices to measure variations in the food supply has led to gross overestimates of the variability of the food supply.

3. The famines that plagued England and France between 1500 and 1800 were man-made – the consequence of failures in the system of food distribution related to an extremely inelastic demand for food inventories rather than to natural calamities or inadequate technology.

4. Not only was it within the power of government to eliminate famines but the food distribution policies of James I and Charles I apparently succeeded in reducing the variability of annual wheat prices by over 70 percent.

5. Although proper governmental policy could have eliminated famines before 1800, it could not have eliminated chronic malnutrition. Elimination of chronic malnutrition required advances

in agricultural and related technologies that permitted the per capita consumption of food to increase by about 50 percent.

6. Improvements in average nutritional status (as indicated by stature and BMIs) appear to explain over 80 percent of the decline in mortality rates in England, France, and Sweden between 18-IV and 19-III but only about half of the mortality decline between 19-III and 20-III.

7. Stunting during developmental ages had a long reach, substantially increasing both morbidity and mortality rates at middle age and later. Small males were at much higher risk of developing chronic diseases during ages twenty-three to forty and were at much higher risk of death over age forty-nine, even if they had optimal BMIs.

These findings indicate that the elimination of chronic malnutrition played a large role in the secular improvement in health and life expectancy. They also suggest that the elimination of stunting at early ages is of major importance in the reduction of morbidity and mortality rates in middle age and later. Optimizing the BMI at mature ages may reduce some risks faced by stunted adults, but it does not eliminate the effects of stunting. It also appears that the optimal BMI may be higher for stunted than for tall adults.

### APPENDIX

This appendix deals with the assumptions, mathematical derivations, estimation procedures, and sources of data for the analysis and estimates presented earlier. (For the assumptions, mathematical derivations, and estimation procedures reported in the sixth section of this chapter, see Fogel 1987.)

The two principal implicit assumptions that underlie the analysis in the preceding second and third sections are traditional in the literature on the pricing of English grain during the early modern era (here taken to be 1500–1750) and are consistent with the available evidence. The first of these assumptions is that the average price each year was established under conditions of a completely inelastic aggregate short-run supply curve. The second is that year-to-year changes in price were due to fluctuations in this short-run supply from one harvest to another around a fixed (or relatively fixed) aggregate demand curve.

The assumption that the demand curve was relatively fixed rests on the flat trend in income and in the relative prices of complements and substitutes for foodgrains (broadly defined) as well as on the stability of tastes (Drummond and Wilbraham 1958; Mitchell and Deane 1962; Holderness 1976; Coleman 1977; Wrigley and Schofield 1981; Grigg 1982; Shammas 1983).[26] The assumption that the short-run supply curve of grain was completely inelastic rests on (1) the observation that once the harvest was concluded, the production of grain could not be increased until the next crop was planted and harvested, and (2) the fact that the price wedge between England and the Continent was such that net imports of grain were generally negative even during years of dearth. In the few years when net imports were positive, they were about 1 percent of annual consumption (Gras 1915; Barnes 1930; Mitchell and Deane 1962).[27]

When the aggregate short-run supply curve is perfectly inelastic, the usual problems of simultaneity disappear, and the estimate of the elasticity of aggregate demand curve can be obtained by regressing price directly on quantity. However, the usual econometric issues of simultaneity remain if one wishes to explain the distribution of the fixed supply between the holders and nonholders of grain inventories (cf. Fogel and Engerman 1974). That task is not undertaken in the second section. When it is undertaken in the third section, the key parameters are not estimated by the econometric procedures since neither the

---

[26] Wrigley and Schofield (1981) present a twenty-five-year moving average of a real wage index, which they use as a proxy for the trend in real annual per capita income. The average rate of increase in that index between c. 1551 and c. 1751 is about 0.06% per annum. However, during that period, the index trends downward for about seventy-three years beginning c. 1562 and then upward for a longer period beginning c. 1635. The average annual rate of decrease in the population index between 1562 and 1635 is about –0.26%, while the average rate of increase between 1635 and 1750 is about 0.25%.

[27] Annual net exports or imports of grain were convened into a percentage of total annual grain consumption on the assumptions that grains provided 80% of caloric intake and that the average daily per capita consumption of all foods yielded about 2,100 calories. The total of annual calories obtained from grains in a given year was estimated by multiplying the population of a given year by $1.200 \times 0.8 \times 365$. Net exports of grain were convened into calories on the assumption that 29% of the weight of grain was lost in processing (either milling or using grain to produce beer) so that the flour equivalent of a bushel of wheat was about 44 pounds and each pound of equivalent wheat flour provided 1,584 kcal (Mitchell and Deane 1962; McCance and Widdowson 1967). Estimates of the average annual net exports of grain are also provided by Bairoch (1973), Coleman (1977), and Deane and Cole (1969); cf. Chartres (1985).

time series nor the cross-sectional data needed for such estimation are available.

A third important implicit assumption for the analysis presented in the second section is that the distribution of arable land among crops did not vary from year to year but remained fixed by conventions that changed slowly over time. Consequently, all the short-run variation in output from one year to the next in grain crops has traditionally been presumed to have been due to variations in per acre yields rather than to variations in the number of acres sown (Slicher Van Bath 1963; Hoskins 1964, 1968; Appleby 1978; Abel 1980; Grigg 1982; Wrigley 1987).

## The Derivation of Equation (7)

The demand curve for the $i$th class of consumers for a good $(Q)$, when income is measured in real terms, may be written as

$$Q_i = \left( \frac{Y_i}{P^{\beta i} P_m^{1-\beta i}} \right)^{\psi_i} P_m^{\varepsilon_{mi}} P^{-\bar{\varepsilon}_i}, \tag{7a}$$

where

$Q$ = the quantity of grain

$P$ = the price of $Q$

$P_m$ = the price of all other goods, $Q_m$

$Y$ = nominal income

$\beta$ = the share of $Q$ in consumption expenditures

$1 - \beta$ = the share of all other goods in consumption expenditures

$\psi$ = the income elasticity of the demand for $Q$

$\varepsilon_m$ = the cross-elasticity of the demand for $Q$ with respect to $P_m$

$\bar{\varepsilon}$ = the own-price elasticity of the income-adjusted demand for $Q$

$i$ = a subscript referring to the $i$th class of consumers

Differentiating (7a) totally and rearranging terms yields

$$\overset{*}{Q}_i = \psi_i \overset{*}{Y}_i + [\varepsilon_{mi} - \psi_i(1 - \beta_i)] \overset{*}{P}_m - (\psi_i \beta_i + \bar{\varepsilon}_i) \overset{*}{P}. \tag{7b}$$

Since by assumption $Q_m$ is the numeraire, $\overset{*}{P}_m = 0$, and Equation (7b) reduces to

$$\overset{*}{Q}_i = \psi_i \overset{*}{Y}_i - (\psi_i \beta_i + \bar{\varepsilon}_i)\overset{*}{P}. \tag{7c}$$

Now, by definition,

$$Y_i = P Q_i + P_m Q_{mi}. \tag{7d}$$

Differentiating (7d) totally yields

$$\overset{*}{Y}_i = \theta_i(\overset{*}{P} + \overset{*}{Q}_i) + (1 - \theta_i)(\overset{*}{P}_m + \overset{*}{Q}_{mi}), \tag{7e}$$

where $\theta_i$ is the share of $PQ_i$ in $Y_i$. Since $Q_m$ is the numeraire and $\overset{*}{Q}_m = 0$ by assumption, (7e) reduces to

$$\overset{*}{Y}_i = \theta_i(\overset{*}{P} + \overset{*}{Q}_i). \tag{7f}$$

If it is also assumed that all classes that own farmland suffer or benefit from random fluctuations in yields proportionately,

$$\overset{*}{Q}_i = -\varepsilon_t \overset{*}{P}, \tag{7g}$$

so that (7f) reduces to

$$\overset{*}{Y}_i = (1 - \varepsilon_t)\theta_i \overset{*}{P}, \tag{7h}$$

where $\varepsilon_t$ is the aggregate price elasticity of demand over all classes of consumers of grain (see Equation (10)). Substituting (7h) into (7c) and rearranging terms yields

$$\overset{*}{Q}_i = \{\psi_i[\theta_i(1 - \varepsilon_t) - \beta_i] - \bar{\varepsilon}_i\}\overset{*}{P}. \tag{7i}$$

Hence the price elasticity of demand for the $i$th class of consumers ($\varepsilon_i$) is the coefficient of $\overset{*}{P}$ in (7i), or

$$\varepsilon_i = [\theta_i(1 - \varepsilon_t) - \beta_i]\psi_i - \bar{\varepsilon}_i, \tag{7j}$$

which is the same as Equation (7).

## The Derivation of Equations (8) and (10)

The derivation of Equation (8) follows directly from the identity

$$Q_c = Q_1 + Q_2 + Q_3 + Q_4 = \sum_{i=1}^{4} Q_i, \qquad (8a)$$

where

$Q_c$ = the aggregate demand for foodgrains

$Q_1, Q_2, Q_3, Q_4$ = demand for foodgrains of each of four classes defined in Table 3.5

Differentiating (8a) totally yields

$$\overset{*}{Q_c} = \sum_{i=1}^{4} \varphi_i \overset{*}{Q_i}, \qquad (8b)$$

where

$\varphi_i$ = the share of $Q_i$ in $Q_c$

Substituting $-\varepsilon_i \overset{*}{P}$ for $\overset{*}{Q_i}$ in (8b) yields

$$\overset{*}{Q_c} = -\overset{*}{P} \sum_{i=1}^{4} \varphi_i \overset{*}{Q_i}. \qquad (8c)$$

Hence, by definition, we have

$$\varepsilon_c = \sum_{i=1}^{4} \varphi_i \varepsilon_i = \varphi_1 \varepsilon_1 + \varphi_2 \varepsilon_2 + \varphi_3 \varepsilon_3 + \varphi_4 \varepsilon_4, \qquad (8d)$$

which is the same as Equation (8).

The derivation of Equation (10) is symmetrical to the derivation for Equation (8), except that the initial identity is

$$Q_t = Q_c + Q_s \qquad (10a)$$

where

$Q_t$ = the aggregate quantity demanded for grain for all uses

$Q_s$ = the quantity demanded for grain used as seed, feed, and carryover inventories

## The Sources for the Estimation of Parameters in Equations
### (4), (5), (6), and (11)

The estimate for $\sigma_q$ was obtained by fitting a normal distribution to the ratio of the residuals to trend values of annual wheat yields obtained from a linear regression of yields on time. Per acre yields, rather than annual wheat production or wheat production plus net imports, were used because of the assumption in the literature that the distribution of arable land across crops remained fixed from year to year by conventions that changed only very slowly over time. The estimated standard deviation of the residuals around yields is greater than those around the production or around the annual production plus net imports. The data on wheat yields for the period 1884–1913 are from Mitchell and Deane (1962). The root mean square errors around quadratic trends were lower than those around the linear trends.

The estimates of $\alpha$ were based on two time series of prices that were spliced at the overlap to provide a continuous series for the period 1540–1738. The series for 1540–1649 are from Bowden (1967), and the series for 1640–1749 are from Bowden (1985). "Grains" was defined to include wheat, barley, oats, rye, and peas and beans. "Food" was defined to include the preceding crops plus livestock and animal products. The grain price index and the food price index were constructed by giving equal weight to the prices of each of the commodities. The reasons for choosing equal weights are discussed by Bowden (1967). Plausible alternative weighting schemes (such as those indicated in Phelps Brown and Hopkins 1956; Shammas 1983; Thirsk 1983; Shammas 1988; and Komlos 1988) tend to reduce both $\alpha$ and $\sigma_{gp}$ because the prices of livestock and animal products are less variable than those of grains. The data on crop yields and total output are reported in Mitchell and Deane (1962) and in the sources cited there.

The standard deviations of prices from trend during 1540–1738 were computed around a twenty-five-year moving average in which the trend value of the price was standardized at 1. A similar procedure was followed in computing the standard deviation around a moving average of the real wage series developed by Wrigley and Schofield (1981) from the series of Phelps Brown and Hopkins as well as around the original price series. The estimates of standard deviation around trend from these series over 1541–1871 were quite close to those computed from the Bowden all-food series for 1540–1738. Use of an eleven-year moving average instead of a twenty-five-year moving average also had negligible effects on the estimates of the standard deviation around trend in the several series.

### Sources for the Parameter Estimates in Table 3.5

*Column 1.* The population shares are based on King's table (Laslett 1984), except that out-servants were divided among the top three classes on the assumption that there were an average of five out-servants for each household of a landlord ("landlords" include the gentry down through "Persons in the Law") and an average of 0.44 out-servants for each farm and lesser landlord households in the category of shopkeepers, minor professionals, and craftsmen (including military officers). The remainder of the households in King's table, which comprise the fourth class of Table 3.5, are presumed to hire no out-servants. The analysis stemming from the table is not particularly sensitive to reasonable alternative definitions of classes or of other distributions of out-servants, nor to reestimates of King's table like the one proposed by Lindert and Williamson (1982), since such redistribution would have little effect on the inequality of the caloric distribution by income or social class.

*Column 2.* The shares of the four classes are based on the assumption that the English distribution of calories was lognormal with $\bar{x} = 2.700$ kcal per equivalent adult and $s/\bar{x} = 0.3$ (see Table 3.8). The means of the four classes are obtained from

$$Z_{mi} = \frac{N_i}{(2\pi)^{0.5}} \int_{Z_i}^{z_{i+j}} Z e^{-0.5 Z^2} dz \qquad \text{(A1)}$$

$$\bar{X}_i = e^{S_{mi}\sigma + \mu} \qquad \text{(A2)}$$

where

$Z_{mi}$ = the $Z$ scores of the mean of the $i$th class

$Z_{j+i}$ and $Z_i$ = the $Z$ scores of the upper and lower bounds of the interval for the $i$th class

TABLE 3.10. *Assumed Shares of Grain in Class-Specific Expenditure*

| Class | (1) Share of Food in Total Expenditure | (2) Share of Grain in Food Expenditure | (3) (1) × (2) |
|---|---|---|---|
| 1 | 0.30 | 0.50 | 0.15 |
| 2 | 0.40 | 0.40 | 0.15 |
| 3 | 0.60 | 0.60 | 0.35 |
| 4 | 0.80 | 0.90 | 0.70 |

$\overline{X_i}$ = the mean of the $i$th interval in the lognormal distribution

$N_i$ = the reciprocal of the area between $Z_i$ and $Z_{i+j}$

*Column 3.* The share of grain in the expenditure of the four classes is based on the assumptions listed in Table 3.10. Values in column 3 were rounded to the nearest 5 percent. These estimates are rough approximations based on data in Phelps Brown and Hopkins (1956), Stigler (1974), Crafts (1980), and Shammas (1983, 1984) (cf. Thirsk 1983). The share of grain and of food in total expenditures for landlords may seem high, but it should be kept in mind that the majority of the persons in their households were from the lower classes and that bread and beer or ale were the main components of their ration (cf. Dyer 1983).

*Column 4.* Estimates of King (1973) and Davenant (1699) indicate that foodgrains accounted for about 43 percent of value added in agriculture circa 1700, and animal products accounted for about 30 percent (cf. Deane and Cole 1969; O'Brien and Keyder 1978; Chartres 1985). The remaining 27 percent was accounted for by feed crops (e.g., flax, hemp), timber, and firewood. It is likely, however, that nongrain products, particularly animal products, represented a larger share of the agricultural income of wealthy landholders (class 1) than of farmers and lesser landlords (class 2). I have assumed that $1 - \varepsilon_t = -0.82$, that class 1 had claims on or produced about one-quarter of annual grain output, and that the remaining three-quarters belonged to class 2.

*Column 5.* The income elasticity for grains in class 4 was estimated directly by Shammas (1984) from the Eden and Davies' surveys of circa 1790. Her figure (0.92) is quite close to the elasticity of grain (rice)

derived from Timmer's equation for contemporary Indonesia (Timmer et al. 1983). For classes 2 and 3, I used Timmer's equation, and the income per household relatives for classes 2 and 3 was computed from King's table (Laslett 1984), with the per household income of class 4 standardized at 100. Since the relative average income of class 1 was far beyond the range of observations on which Timmer's equation was computed, I arbitrarily assumed that the value of $\psi$ for class 1 was one-half of that for class 2.

*Column 6.* Timmer's procedure (Timmer et al. 1983) was followed, employing the income relatives computed from King's table, as indicated in the preceding paragraph relating to column 5. For the reasons indicated in the previous note, and because of Timmer's finding that $\bar{\varepsilon}$ declines more rapidly than $\psi$ with income, I arbitrarily assumed that $\bar{\varepsilon}$ for class 1 was 0.02.

# 4

## Trends in Physiological Capital

### *Implications for Equity in Health Care*

The health of the general population in previous eras was terrible, but it was especially bad for the lower classes. In the eighteenth century, for example, chronic malnutrition was so severe that the bottom 20 percent of the English income distribution lacked the energy for regular work. From the Elizabethan age to the end of the nineteenth century, one-fifth of the potential English labor force lived out their brief lives as paupers and beggars. These potential workers were excluded from the labor force not because of an inadequate demand for labor, as was the case during the Great Depression of the 1930s, but because they lacked entitlements to food. The situation in France and the rest of Western Europe was even worse than in England. Prior to the twentieth century, chronic malnutrition was the fate of the majority of the population.

The problem was not only that most of the population of Western Europe lacked adequate amounts of energy for work but also that their food supply was typically too small to allow for their proper physiological development. Energy available for work is a residual. It is the difference between the food metabolized (chemically transformed so that its energy is available for use by the body) and the energy that the body requires for baseline maintenance. Baseline maintenance has two components. The larger component, the basal metabolic rate (or BMR), accounts for about four-fifths of baseline maintenance. BMR is the amount of energy needed to maintain body temperature and to keep the heart and other vital organs functioning when the body is completely at rest. The other 20 percent of baseline maintenance is the energy needed to digest food and for vital hygiene (defecating, urinating, washing). It does not include the energy needed to prepare a meal or to clean the kitchen afterward.

The amount of energy required for baseline maintenance depends on an individual's size. The typical American male today in his thirties is about 69.7 inches tall and weighs about 172 pounds. Such a male requires daily about 1,794 calories for basal metabolism and a total of 2,279 calories for baseline maintenance. If either the British or the French had been that large during the eighteenth century, virtually all of the energy produced by their food supplies would have been required for maintenance, and hardly any would have been available to sustain work. The relatively small food supplies available to produce the national products of these two countries around 1700 suggest that the typical adult male must have been quite short and very light. This inference is supported by data on stature and weight that have been collected for European nations.[1]

PHYSIOLOGICAL CAPITAL

Individuals who are stunted and wasted are at much higher risk of developing chronic disabilities early and dying prematurely. Over the past three centuries, human beings in Organisation for Economic Co-operation and Development (OECD) countries have increased their average body weight by over 50 percent and their average longevity by over 100 percent, and they have greatly improved the robustness and capacity of vital organ systems. I shall refer to this enhanced physiological capacity as *physiological capital.*

Physiological capital is a relatively new concept for economists. It differs from, but is related to, the better known concepts of human capital and health capital. The *human* capital concept was developed to explain differences in earnings by occupation, over the life cycle, by industries and by regions. It focuses especially on the contribution of education (including on-the-job training) to an individual's stock of human capital and to the rate of return on investments in education. The *health* capital concept was developed to explain the demand for goods and services that offsets the depreciation in the initial

[1] See Table 3.9.

endowment of health over the life cycle. Although health capital presupposes physiological capital, it does not deal with it explicitly. Health capital assumes the health stock with which each individual is born and considers how investment in health care can reduce the rate of depreciation in that stock. It does not address why some people have a greater initial stock than others, and it does not recognize the relationship between the size of the initial stock and its rate of depreciation. Nor does it take notice of the effect of the date of birth on the size of the initial stock or on the rate of depreciation. In other words, it does not confront the issue of how the average initial stock of physiological capital has been changing from one generation to another. However, all these issues are central to the concept of physiological capital.

Since the beginning of the eighteenth century, physiological capital has been accumulating very rapidly. Much of this improvement is the result of a process that Dora Costa and I have called technophysio evolution, a synergism between technological advances and physical improvements that has produced a form of human evolution that is biological but not genetic, rapid, culturally transmitted, and not necessarily stable. This process is still ongoing in both rich and developing countries.

The rapid accumulation of physiological capital is tied both to long-term reductions in environmental hazards and to the conquest of chronic malnutrition (made possible by technophysio evolution), and it is reflected in the improvements in stature and the body mass index, a measure of weight standardized for height.

Variations in height and weight are associated with variations in the chemical composition of the tissues that make up vital organs, in the quality of the electrical transmission across membranes, and in the functioning of the endocrine system and other vital systems. Nutritional status, as reflected in height and weight, thus appears to be a critical link connecting improvements in technology to improvements in human physiology.

Research on this connection is developing rapidly, but the exact mechanisms by which malnutrition and trauma in utero or in early childhood are transformed into organ dysfunctions are still unclear. What is agreed on is that the basic structure of most organs is laid down early, and it is reasonable to infer that poorly developed organs may break down earlier than well-developed ones. The principal evidence so far is statistical, and despite agreement on certain specific dysfunctions, there is no generally accepted theory of cellular aging (Tanner 1990, 1993).

With these caveats in mind, recent research bearing on the connection between malnutrition and body size and the later onset of chronic diseases can conveniently be divided into three categories. The first category involves forms of malnutrition (including the ingestion of toxic substances) that cause permanent, promptly visible physiological damage, as is seen in the impairment of the nervous systems of fetuses due to excessive smoking or consumption of alcohol by pregnant women. Protein-calorie malnutrition in infancy and early childhood can lead to a permanent impairment of central nervous system function. Folate and iodine deficiency in utero and moderate to severe iron deficiency during infancy also appear to cause permanent neurological damage (Scrimshaw and Gordon 1968; Chávez et al. 1995).

But not all damage due to retarded development in utero or infancy caused by malnutrition shows up immediately. Barker (1998) and colleagues have reported that such conditions as coronary heart disease, hypertension, stroke, non-insulin-dependent diabetes, and autoimmune thyroiditis begin in utero or in infancy but do not become apparent until mid-adult or later ages. In these cases, individuals appear to be in good health and function well in the interim. However, early onset of the degenerative diseases of old age is linked to inadequate cellular development early in life.

Certain physiological dysfunctions incurred by persons suffering from malnutrition can, in principle, be reversed by improved dietary intake, but they often persist because the cause of the malnutrition persists. If the malnutrition persists long enough, these conditions can become irreversible or fatal. This category of consequences includes the degradation of tissue structure, especially in such vital organs as the lungs, the heart, and the gastrointestinal tract. In the case of the gastrointestinal system, atrophy of the mucosal cells and intestinal villi results in decreased absorption of nutrients. Malnutrition also has been related to impairment of immune function, increased susceptibility to infections, poor wound healing, electrolyte imbalances, endocrine imbalances, and, in adults, dangerous cardiac arrhythmias and increased chronic rheumatoid disorders (McMahon and Bistrian 1990).

So far, I have focused on the contribution of improved nutrition and technological change to physiological improvement. However, the process has been synergistic, with improvement in nutrition and physiology contributing significantly to the process of economic growth and technological progress. For example, technophysio evolution appears to account for about half of British economic growth over the past two centuries. Much of this gain was due to the improvement in human thermodynamic efficiency: since 1790, the rate of converting human energy input into work output appears to have increased by about 50 percent (Fogel 1994).

## EQUITY IMPLICATIONS OF THE ACCUMULATION OF PHYSIOLOGICAL CAPITAL

The process of accumulating physiological capital has had an effect on health care by *reducing* socioeconomic disparities in the burden of disease. I emphasize the word *reducing* because though many recent epidemiological studies in OECD nations find strong relationships between socioeconomic variables and health status, these relationships are what is left of a nexus that used to be much stronger than it is today.

The progress toward greater equity in health status between 1800 and the second half of the twentieth century is illustrated by Figure 4.1. The lines on this graph are normal approximations of the frequency distributions of birth weights. Birth weight is represented on the vertical axis, and the horizontal axis represents $z$-scores (deviations of birth weight from the mean measured in units of the standard deviations). Hence the cumulative frequency distribution is represented by a straight line. The lowest line represents the distribution of nonwhites in the United States in 1950. These newborns had a mean birth weight of 3,218 grams, and as indicated by Figure 4.1, about 13 percent weighed less than 2,501 grams at birth. The second line is the distribution of birth weights for lower-class women in Bombay (Jayant 1964). The mean birth weight in this population was just 2,525 grams. In this case, nearly half (46%) of the births were below the critical level, although the women in the sample were not the poorest of the poor.

The third curve is the probable distribution of the birth weights of the children of impoverished English workers about 1800. The distribution of the birth weights in this class around 1800 probably had a

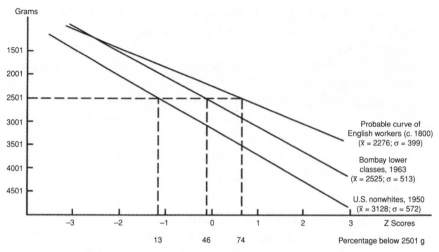

FIGURE 4.1. The percentage of male births with weights below 2,501 grams in two modern populations and of poor English workers during the early nineteenth century.

mean of 2,276 grams, which is about 249 grams (about half a pound) below the average in the deliveries of the lower-class women in Bombay. It follows that about 79 percent of the births among impoverished English workers around 1800 were below 2,501 grams.

The implication of this distribution of birth weights is revealed by Table 4.1. Column 2 represents the actual schedule of neonatal death rates by weight for nonwhite U.S. males in 1950, and column 3 gives the actual distribution of their birth weights. The product of these two columns yields a neonatal death rate of 26.8 per 1,000. If, however, this U.S. population had had the distribution of the birth weights of the impoverished English workers of 1800 (column 4), their neonatal death rates would have been 173.0 per thousand. The implication of Table 4.1 is that improvements in nutrition sufficient to have shifted the mean birth weight from 2,276 grams to 3,128 grams would have reduced the infant death rate by 83 percent.

Figure 4.1 reflects an important intergenerational influence on health before the era of cesarean sections and neonatal intensive care units. Malnourished mothers produced small children not only because of deficiencies in their diets and exposure to disease during pregnancy but also because their short stature was associated with small pelvic

TABLE 4.1. *Effects of Shift in Distribution of Birth Weights on Neonatal Death Rate, Holding Schedule of Death Rates (by Weight) Constant*

| Weight (grams) | Neonatal Death Rate of Singleton Nonwhite U.S. Males in 1950 (per 1,000) | Distribution of Birth Weights of Singleton, Nonwhite U.S. Males in 1950 with $\bar{x}$ 3,128 SD = 572 g | Distribution of Birth Weights in Population with $\bar{x}$ 2,276 SD = 399 g |
|---|---|---|---|
| ≤1,500 | 686.7 | 0.0117 | 0.1339 |
| 1,501–2,000 | 221.3 | 0.0136 | 0.2421 |
| 2,001–2,500 | 62.1 | 0.0505 | 0.3653 |
| 2,501–3,000 | 19.7 | 0.1811 | 0.2198 |
| 3,001–3,500 | 10.7 | 0.351 | 0.0372 |
| 3,501–4,000 | 12.1 | 0.2599 | 0.0017 |
| 4,001–4,500 | 13 | 0.0865 | |
| ≥4,501 | 23.2 | 0.0456 | |
| Neonatal Death Rate (per 1,000) | | 26.8 | 173.0 (implied) |

*Sources:* Columns 2 and 3: U.S. National Office of Vital Statistics (1954); column 4: see Fogel (1986b, nos. 21, 23, 24, and 26).

cavities. As a result, the birth weight that minimized perinatal deaths was about 700 grams below that of the U.S. women referred to in Figure 4.1. In other words, a condition for surviving the birth process was such a low birth weight that the neonate was at high risk of dying shortly after birth. The escape from that dilemma is now almost universal in OECD nations. Poor women have accumulated physiological capital at an intergenerational rate that was rapid enough to shift the birth weight of their children to a range that is about 1.7 times what it was two centuries ago. This means that less than 8 percent of all births in OECD nations are now below 2,501 grams (Wilcox et al. 1995; Graafmans et al. 2002; Martin et al. 2002).

Further evidence of the secular trend toward the more equal distribution of physiological capital over the past two centuries comes from the changes in adult heights among the British. Data collected on the stature of the British upper classes, together with data on the lower classes, make it possible to estimate how much of the improvement in the average stature in Great Britain between 1820 and 1978 was due to a closing of the gap between the upper and lower classes and how much was due to an upward shift in attainable average height.

By "attainable," I mean not genetically attainable but, within genetic constraints, attainable under the most favorable prevailing socioeconomic circumstances. It appears that approximately three-quarters of the increase in the mean final heights of British males since about 1820 was due to the decrease in class differentials in height and the balance to an upward shift in the mean final heights of the upper class (which may be taken as a measure of the attainable mean height at any point in time) (Floud et al. 1990). In this connection, it is worth noting that Sweden and Norway, which have relatively low after-tax Gini ratios (an index of income concentration), also have low height differentials by socioeconomic class. The means of adult height in these nations now exceed those of nations with relatively high Gini ratios, such as the United States and Great Britain, by several centimeters (Kuh et al. 1991; Cavelaars et al. 2000; Fredriks et al. 2000; World Bank 2002).

What can be said about the factors responsible for the rapid increase in the national stocks of physiological capital in OECD countries and for its more equal distribution? The central scientific issue is, how much of the improvement in physiological capital is due to improvements in the environment, especially between the 1880s and the end of World War II, and how much is due to advances in medical technology and the development of effective systems for delivering health services. These two aspects of the accumulation of physiological capital are not neatly separated because physicians and biochemists played a large role in environmental improvements. Moreover, some important steps in the improvement of the environment, such as the draining of swamps, were by-products of the growth of agriculture, while others awaited the development of new technologies for urban waste disposal. Measurement of the relative importance of these and other factors – such as improvements in the diversity and year-round supply of food – to the accelerated accumulation of human capital is still elusive, partly because of the complex interactions that are involved but mainly because of the absence of a database containing information on the relevant explanatory variables.

Although much was done to eliminate environmental barriers to the enhancement of physiological capital during the twentieth century, the process of improvement is not yet complete because environmental factors still contribute to low birth weight. As a result, deficiencies in physiological capital continue to influence health status and rates of the deterioration in health over the life cycle. Studies of a British cohort born in 1958 reveal that low-birth-weight children were not only stunted at maturity (by about 2 inches compared to children of optimal birth weight) but were also disadvantaged in their cognitive development, as reflected in school performance, and these deficiencies were aggravated by the social class of their parents at the time of birth (Teranishi et al. 2001; Jefferis et al. 2002). Some of the problems persisted even after the emergence of neonatal intensive care units in the 1970s (Hack et al. 2002). Studies also show that low-birth-weight children also have elevated risks of behavioral problems, psychiatric disorders, linguistic defects, and motor disabilities (Yliherva et al. 2001; Elgen et al. 2002). Although recent advances in neonatal technology appear to be improving long-term outcomes, they have not eliminated the need to confront continuing environmental hazards (McCormick and Richardson 2002).

## IMPLICATIONS OF ENHANCED PHYSIOLOGICAL CAPITAL FOR EGALITARIAN HEALTH POLICIES

The substantial role played by secular enhancement in physiological capital has a number of implications for those concerned with designing policies to reduce inequities in health status by socioeconomic class. Since research bearing on secular trends in health status and the factors responsible for the decline in disabilities over the course of the twentieth century is still at an early stage, I will summarize my current views as a set of theses.

### Thesis 1: Environmental Improvement Is More Important than Access to Health Care

The more egalitarian health status that exists today is due primarily to environmental improvements that enhanced the physiological capital of successive cohorts rather than to greater access to health care services. Support for this proposition can be found in a series of recent studies that have linked events early in life, including the intrauterine period, to the onset of chronic conditions at middle and late ages.

The strongest evidence for such links pertain to hypertension and coronary heart disease (Cresswell et al. 1997; Scrimshaw 1997; Barker 1998). A review of thirty-two papers dealing with the relationship between birth weight and hypertension showed a tendency for blood pressure in middle age to increase as birth weight declines (Law and Shiell 1996). Evidence of a connection between birth size and later coronary heart disease has been found in England, Wales, Finland, Sweden, and India (Frankel et al. 1996; Stein et al. 1996; Forsén et al. 1997; Koupilová et al. 1997).

The theory of a nexus between environmental insults in utero or at early postnatal ages and the risk of chronic health conditions half a century or more later calls attention to the rapid improvement in the environment between 1890 and 1940 to which I have already alluded. This period also witnessed improvements in the diversity of the food supply throughout the year and the beginnings of dietary supplements that increased year-round consumption of vitamins and other trace elements. The importance of year-round nutrition has been underscored by two recent studies that have shown strong correlations between month of birth and the longevity of middle-aged men in Austria, Denmark, Australia, and the United States; the results reflected differences in the availability of food to pregnant mothers over the seasons (Doblhammer and Vaupel 2001; Kanjanapipatkul 2001). These developments largely preceded the revolution in health care services that followed World War II.

Further evidence that a substantial part of the improvement in health status during the twentieth century was not due to direct medical care is provided by Table 4.2, which shows that the proportion of white males who were still free of chronic conditions between ages fifty and sixty-nine was substantially higher in the mid-1990s than a century earlier. This improvement could not be due primarily to the curative interventions of health care providers with persons already afflicted with chronic diseases because we are looking only at the subset of people who were not yet afflicted by chronic diseases. Table 4.3 shows that for those who did develop four common chronic diseases, the average age of onset for men who reached age sixty-five in the 1980s or later was between seven and eleven years later than for those who reached age sixty-five in 1910 or earlier (see Costa 2000).

TABLE 4.2. *The Increase in the Proportion of White Males without Chronic Conditions, during the Course of the Twentieth Century*

| | Proportion without Chronic Conditions | |
|---|---|---|
| Age Interval (years) | 1890–1910 | c. 1994 |
| 50–54 | 0.33 | 0.41 |
| 55–59 | 0.21 | 0.29 |
| 60–64 | 0.1 | 0.25 |
| 65–69 | 0.03 | 0.14 |

*Sources:* Column 2: based on examinations of physicians (http://www.cpe.uchicago.edu/); column 3: Health and Retirement Study surveys 1 and 2, based on recall of previous diagnoses of physicians (http://hrsonline.isr.umich.edu/).

## Thesis 2: Slowed Physiological Capital Depreciation Rates Are More Important than Improved Medical Technology

Although the more extensive and more effective medical interventions of the last third of the twentieth century have contributed to the enhancement of the physiological capital of successive birth cohorts, modern medicine's main contribution has been to slow down the rate of depreciation in the stock of the enhanced physiological capital that the members of these cohorts accumulated during development. This distinction between the increasingly enhanced physiological capital of

TABLE 4.3. *Average Age of Onset of Some Chronic Conditions among American Males Near the Beginning and Near the End of the Twentieth Century*

| Condition | Men Born 1830–1845 | Men Born 1918–1927 |
|---|---|---|
| Heart disease | 55.9 | 65.4 |
| Arthritis | 53.7 | 64.7 |
| Neoplasm | 59.0 | 66.6 |
| Respiratory | 53.8 | 65.0 |

*Sources:* Column 2: Union Army veterans; column 3: Health and Retirement Study surveys 1 and 3.

successive cohorts and those health care interventions that retard the rate of depreciation in a cohort's initial stocks of physiological capital is what is overlooked in the conventional theory of health capital. As a result, the extent of the increase in physiological capital has been underestimated, and this may explain why some economists have tended to slight the role of improving environmental factors and to attribute all of the decline in morbidity and mortality during recent decades to improved medical technology.

Moreover, while it may be true that health care providers have directed their efforts at reducing the rate of deterioration in health, physicians have also significantly contributed to the enhancement of physiological capital. Important steps have included encouraging appropriate behavior by pregnant women, administering nutritional supplements, correcting birth defects, and treating a variety of diseases that interfere with normal growth patterns during developmental ages.

### Thesis 3: Neonatal Environment Is Crucial for Later Health

The evidence currently in hand points to the importance of prenatal care and environmental issues both in enhancing physiological capital and in affecting the rate of depreciation in that capital. In this context, the word *environment* has a dual meaning: the uterus is a crucial environment for the developing embryo and fetus, and the quality of the external environment has an effect on the environmental quality of the uterus. Pregnant women exposed to high levels of pathogens and suffering, for example, from frequent bouts of diarrhea, will have intrauterine environments that retard the development of the children they are bearing. Studies in underdeveloped countries have revealed that the neonates of women who suffered from diarrhea were lighter, and at higher risk of perinatal mortality, than those of mothers who escaped the disease during their pregnancies (Mata 1978; Martorell and Habicht 1986).

Neonatal care and early postnatal care present opportunities for physicians to affect the enhancement of the physiological capital. Providing nutritionally stressed pregnant women with such supplements as folate and iodine will not only reduce the rate of spontaneous abortions but also will reduce the risk of permanent damage to the central nervous system; counseling pregnant women to avoid smoking and alcohol consumption during pregnancy can reduce a major cause of low birth weight and of perinatal mortality; and effective measures to promote breast-feeding can substantially reduce morbidity and mortality among infants who are bottle fed (Forste et al. 2001).

## Thesis 4: Lifestyle Change Is Key to Improving Health

From the standpoint of health equity, the most important issue today in rich nations is not the cleaning up of the environment, as it was a century ago, but the reformation of lifestyle. Practices that undermine the accumulation of physiological capital (such as bottle-feeding instead of breast-feeding infants) or that accelerate the depreciation of physiological capital (such as use of recreational drugs, smoking, excessive alcohol consumption, and overeating) are more frequently practiced among the poor and the poorly educated than among the rich and the well-educated sectors of the population.

As with the public health reforms a century ago, the campaign to change lifestyle in ways that promote the accumulation of physiological capital and retard its depreciation must be a joint venture between government authorities, the private sector (including commercial and voluntary organizations), and health providers. The local level is the key arena for government operations, not only because conditions and issues vary from one locality to another but also because education in the school system is a key site in the campaign to change lifestyles. The joint-venture tactic also applies to cooperation between churches and secular authorities because of the vast pool of potential volunteers for mentoring those suffering from detrimental lifestyles. And the tactic applies to the government and commercial sectors because businesses, including the media, are needed both to propagate healthy lifestyles and to enforce them in the workplace.

Health care providers are needed not only because of their expertise in helping to formulate public policies but also because teaching patients about lifestyle issues is one of their central missions. Doctors play a crucial role in helping patients to implement changes in lifestyle that are promoted in the media and taught in the schools. Moreover, specific treatments are required for those deeply addicted to drugs, excessive eating (or excessive dieting), and other detrimental lifestyles.

### Thesis 5: Health Care Outreach Programs Are More Important than Extension of Insurance

Greater access to clinical care is a high priority in promoting greater health equity, but implementing this goal requires new approaches. It is not enough to wait for poor and poorly educated individuals to seek out available services. Outreach programs need to be developed for the needy, making use of a variety of community organizations already engaged in outreach for other purposes. In this connection, local officials should consider the reintroduction into public schools, particularly those in poor neighborhoods, of periodic health-screening programs, using nurses and physicians on a contract basis.

To some extent, the focus on the extension of health insurance to the 15 percent of the population not currently covered is a diversion from the effective delivery of health care services to the poor. Severe problems of underserving the poor exist in rich nations with universal national health programs; what is needed is aggressive outreach, including the establishment of public health clinics in underserved poor neighborhoods that can supplement the emergency rooms of regular hospitals, which are frequent providers of routine health care services for the poor. Convenient access is a key issue because even individuals with insurance, such as those on Medicaid, may fail to take advantage of available facilities if they are inconvenient. Basements of churches and space in public schools after normal teaching hours can be good locations for community clinics, both because they help to stretch available funds and because they provide familiar settings.

### CONCLUSION

Physiological capital is still a new concept, and the data sets needed to measure changes in this form of capital have only recently become accessible. As a result, the loci of changes in both time and space are just now being assayed. While much remains to be learned about how changes in the physiological capital of pregnant women have contributed to the decline in infant mortality rates, the analysis in Figure 4.1 and Table 4.1 suggests that the effect has been quite significant.

Work undertaken to date suggests that environmental changes, particularly the synergy between technological and physiological improvements, help to explain not only the increase in life expectancy at age fifty but – as Tables 4.2 and 4.3 indicate – also the delay in the average age of incurring particular chronic conditions and the increased age-specific odds of being free of all chronic conditions after age fifty. As the physiological basis for these changes is identified, forecasts of trends in health care costs will become more reliable.

# 5

# Changes in Disparities and Chronic Diseases through the Course of the Twentieth Century

The main proposition of this chapter is that the extent and the severity of chronic conditions in middle and late ages are to a large extent the outcome of environmental insults at early ages, including in utero. Many of these are due to infectious diseases that occur at young ages. Evidence to support this proposition comes partly from the study being conducted at the University of Chicago and elsewhere on the aging of the Union Army veterans, the Early Indicators project. But it is also supported by other longitudinal studies in the United States and abroad. Some recent studies indicate two-generation effects among humans. Perhaps the most widely cited case involves women who were born or were in gestation during the Dutch famine, which lasted about eight or nine months toward the end World War II and was precipitated by sharp reductions in rations. Although this famine resulted in an elevated perinatal death rate, it was for a long time thought that women who survived and were subsequently well fed were just as healthy as women who were born before the famine or afterward. However, when these women themselves began giving birth, their children had elevated perinatal death rates. Of course, we will still have to wait to see what the effects of the famine will be on the rate of increase in chronic conditions and on longevity at older ages. However, there is evidence that children of mothers who were in the first trimester of gestation when the famine struck and who survived infancy have elevated prevalence of coronary heart disease now that they are in their mid-fifties (Roseboom et al. 2000).

TABLE 5.1. *The Share of Northern White Males of Military Age Unfit for Military Service in 1861*

| Age (years) | Cohort Examined (%) | Examinees Who Were Rejected (%) |
|---|---|---|
| 16–19 | 80.9 | 16.0 |
| 20–24 | 70.4 | 24.5 |
| 25–29 | 52.3 | 35.8 |
| 30–34 | 41.0 | 42.9 |
| 35–39 | 41.6 | 52.9 |

Environmental conditions were far more severe during the beginning of the twentieth century, and differences in exposure to disease varied sharply by socioeconomic group. For example, the infant death rate from diarrheal diseases during the summer months in Chicago in 1910 for foreign-born mothers was nine times as high as the rate for native-born mothers (Bridges 2002).

I began this chapter by focusing on infectious diseases because one of the principal findings of the Early Indicators project is that insults from infectious diseases at early ages have a large impact on the prevalence rates of chronic diseases and disabilities in middle and late ages. Another major finding of the project is that the age-specific prevalence rates of chronic diseases were much lower at the end of the twentieth century than they were at the beginning of that century or during the last half of the nineteenth century. The Union Army data reveal the ubiquity of chronic health conditions during the century before World War II. Not only was the overall prevalence rate of these diseases much higher among the elderly than today, but they afflicted the teens, young adults, and middle ages to a much greater extent than today. This fact is brought out by Table 5.1, which shows that more than 80 percent of all males aged sixteen to nineteen in 1861 and more than 70 percent of men aged twenty to twenty-four were examined for the Union Army. These examinees were overwhelmingly volunteers (less than 4% were drafted), who presumably thought they were fit enough to serve. Yet disability rates were higher than today. Even among teenagers, more than one of six was disabled, and among men age thirty-five to thirty-nine, more than half were disabled. Despite their relatively young ages, cardiovascular diseases (mainly rheumatic) accounted for

11 percent of the rejections; hernias another 12 percent; eye, ear, and nose diseases 7 percent; tuberculosis and other respiratory diseases 7 percent; and tooth and gum diseases 8 percent. Most of the other rejections were due to orthopedic conditions and general debility (Lee 2001).

These findings about the early onset of chronic diseases cast new light on the debate about the effect of increased longevity on the prevalence rates of chronic diseases. Those who argued that the effect of increased longevity was to increase the average duration of chronic disease assumed no delay in the average age of onset of these diseases. They were also influenced by cross-sectional evidence that showed some increases in disability rates during the 1970s and 1980s, despite the continuing decline in mortality rates (Riley 1990a; Riley 1990b; Wolfe and Haveman 1990; Riley 1991). It seemed plausible that various health interventions and environmental changes served to reduce the severity of diseases and thus delayed death without providing cures, as has been the case with AIDS.

However, there has been a significant delay in the onset of chronic diseases during the course of the twentieth century (see Table 5.2). Men aged fifty to fifty-four were 24 percent more likely to be free of chronic conditions in 1994 than a century earlier. At age sixty to sixty-four, white males today are 2.5 times more likely to be free of chronic diseases than their counterparts a century ago. Further light is shed on the issue by considering specific diseases (see Table 4.3). Arthritis began eleven years later among men who turned age sixty-five between 1983 and 1992 than among those who turned age sixty-five between 1895 and 1910. The delay in the onset of a chronic condition was about nine years for heart diseases, about eleven years for respiratory diseases (despite much higher rates of cigarette smoking), and nearly eight years for neoplasms.[1]

Union Army veterans who endured poor health did not typically die quickly. Veterans who lived to be at least age fifty, and who entered the pension system before age fifty-one, lived an average of twenty-four

---

[1] Since current techniques make it possible to diagnose heart disease and neoplasms sooner in the development of these diseases than used to be the case c. 1910, the figures given in the text should be considered lower bounds on the delay in the onset of these conditions.

TABLE 5.2. *Average Number of Comorbidities among Veterans Who Lived to Be at Least Age Fifty*

| Average Age of Death (years) | Veterans Who Lived to at Least Age Fifty, Who Died in Interval (%) | Average Number of Comorbidities at Last Examination before Death |
|---|---|---|
| 50–54 | 3.9 | 4 |
| 55–59 | 6.4 | 5 |
| 60–64 | 9.8 | 6 |
| 65–69 | 14 | 6 |
| 70–74 | 18.3 | 7 |
| 75–79 | 19.1 | 7 |
| 80–84 | 15.5 | 7 |
| 85–89 | 9.0 | 8 |
| 90–94 | 3.4 | 8 |
| 95 or over | 0.7 | 7 |

years past age fifty. Moreover, at their last examination on or before age fifty-one, their average degree of disability was 58 percent, where 100 percent indicates complete incapacity for manual labor. Between ages fifty and sixty, disability ratings (controlled for age at death) continued to rise sharply and then increased at a decreasing rate. It is worth noting that of the veterans who lived to be age fifty, about 29 percent lived to be age eighty or more. For these old old, the level of disability for manual labor averaged between 85 and 100 percent for a decade or more. Indeed, some survived with such high levels of disability for as much as a quarter of a century (Helmchen 2003). As Table 5.2 shows, survivors usually acquired more and more comorbidities (the coexistence of two or more disease processes) as they aged. Those who lived past age eighty-five had twice as many comorbidities as those who died by age fifty-five.

Consideration of the sweep of the twentieth century puts the debate over the relationship between the increase in life expectancy and the change in the burden of chronic disease among the elderly in a new perspective. It now appears that the decline in morbidity rates paralleled the decline in mortality rates. Indeed, the delay in the onset of chronic disabilities between 1900 and the 1990s for those who lived to age fifty was greater than the increase in life expectancy at age fifty over the same periods. The average delay in the onset of chronic conditions over the century was more than ten years (Helmchen 2003).[2] However, the average increase in male life expectancy was about 6.6 years (Bell et al. 1992).

Public health policies before 1940 had a large impact on the decline in chronic disability rates decades later. Dora Costa (2000) has estimated the impact of public health and socioeconomic status factors at late developmental and young adult ages on risks of incurring chronic conditions at middle and late ages. Significant predictors included mortality rates in counties of enlistment, infectious diseases experienced during the Civil War, and being a prisoner of war. She focused on a set of chronic conditions for which clinical diagnoses were essentially the same in the early 1900s as today (such as lower back pain, joint problems, decreased breath or adventitious sounds, irregular pulse, and valvular heart disease). This procedure permitted her to estimate how much of the observed decline in the prevalence rates of comparable conditions was due to the reduction in specific risk factors. Prevalence rates for 1971–1980 were computed from the National Health and Nutrition Examination Survey (NHANES).

Costa found that elimination of exposure to specific infectious diseases during developmental and young adult ages explained between 10 and 25 percent of the declines in the specified chronic diseases of middle and late ages between 1900–1910 and 1971–1980. Occupational shifts were also important, accounting for 15 percent of the decline in joint problems, 75 percent of the decline in back pains, and 25 percent of the decline in respiratory diseases.

Costa (2002) pushed this line of analysis further by documenting the decline in functional limitations among U.S. men between ages fifty and seventy-four over the course of the twentieth century. A central issue is the factoring of the decline in functional limitations among three processes: the decline in the prevalence rates of specific chronic diseases, the reduction in the debilitating sequelae of these diseases, and the influence of new medical technologies that relieve and control the

---

[2] The delay in the average age of onset in chronic diseases can be decomposed into two parts: (1) the shift in the age-specific disease schedule and (2) the change in the distribution of ages due to the increase in life expectancy and the decline in the fertility rate. We have not yet completed this decomposition; however, preliminary estimates indicate that the contribution of the change in the age distribution was small.

sequelae. Her analysis turned on five functional limitations: difficulty walking, difficulty bending, paralysis, blindness in at least one eye, and deafness in at least one ear. Prevalence rates of these limitations among men aged fifty to seventy-four were computed for the Union Army, NHANES (1988–1994), and NHIS (1988–1994).

On average, these five functional limitations declined by about 40 percent during the course of the twentieth century. Using probit regressions, Costa attributed 24 percent of the decline to reduction in the debilitating effect of chronic conditions and 37 percent to the reduced rates of chronic conditions.

### THE SIGNIFICANCE OF CHANGES IN BODY SIZE

The contribution of improvements in body size as measured by stature, body mass index (BMI), and other dimensions has run through the research of the Early Indicators project like a red line. The discovery of correlations in time series going back to the colonial period between changes in stature and changes in life expectancy for the United States was reported first in 1986, although it was known as early as 1978.[3] Pursuit of a variety of issues called attention to the significance of changes in body size to the long-term decline in chronic conditions and mortality. For example, Diane Lauderdale and Paul Rathouz (1999) sought to investigate the impact of unhealthy environments on the genetic component of height. They hypothesized that an unhealthy environment might attenuate the effects of genotype, and to test that hypothesis, they constructed a sample of brothers who served in the Union Army. Their analysis showed that brothers from unhealthy counties had both higher variances in height and lower covariance in the heights of siblings than was expected from standard equations for measuring genetic influences in the heights of siblings. Study of the likelihood of developing specific diseases while in service also pointed to the importance of stature. For example, short recruits were more likely to develop tuberculosis while in service than taller ones (Birchenall 2003; see also Lee 1997).

---

[3] For reviews of earlier work dealing with the use of height, BMI, and other anthropometric measures as indexes of changes in health and the standard of living over time, see Steckel (1995) and Komlos and Cuff (1998).

In 1995, Dora Costa discovered a sample of twenty-three thousand Union Army recruits who were, for scientific reasons, more intensively examined than the typical recruit (Costa 2004). Benjamin A. Gould, a leading astronomer and one of the founders of the National Academy of Sciences, who was in charge of the project, collected information on waist and hip circumference, lifting strength, vital capacity of lungs, height, weight, shoulder breadth, and chest circumference. The sample covered whites, blacks, and Native Americans. Costa linked a subsample of 521 white recruits who survived to 1900 to their pension records. She also compared the Union Army soldiers with soldiers measured in 1946–1947, 1950, and 1988. Over a span of one hundred years, men in the military became taller and heavier. Their height increased by 5 cm, and the BMIs of men aged thirty-one to thirty-five increased from 23 to 26. Controlling for BMI and age, the waist-to-hip and chest-to-shoulder ratios (both measures of abdominal fat) were significantly greater in the Gould sample than in the 1950 and 1988 samples.

Using an independent competing risk hazard model to estimate the effect of changes in body shape on the risk of death from cerebrovascular and ischemic heart disease at older ages, Costa found that a low waist-to-hip ratio increased mortality by 4.4 times relative to the mean and controlling for BMI, while a high waist-to-hip ratio increased mortality risk by 2.9 times. Substituting the characteristics of soldiers in 1950 (who reached age sixty-five or over during the late 1980s) into her regression model produced a 15 percent decline in all-cause mortality above age sixty-four, implying that changes in frame size explain about 47 percent of the total decline in all-cause mortality at older ages between the beginning and the end of the twentieth century.

## THE THEORY OF TECHNOPHYSIO EVOLUTION

Recognition of environmentally induced changes in human physiology during the twentieth century that had a profound impact on the process of aging did not become apparent to Early Indicators project investigators until mid-1993. The key finding was that prevalence rates of the main chronic diseases among Union Army veterans aged sixty-five and older were much higher in 1910 than among veterans of World War II of the same age during the middle to late 1980s. That finding was first set forth in a 1993 working paper and was elaborated and subsequently characterized as a *theory of technophysio evolution*. The theory of technophysio evolution arose out of intense discussion among the senior investigators, consultants, and research assistants during 1993–1994, with the physicians providing much of the intellectual leadership, especially Nevin Scrimshaw, J. M. Tanner, and Irving Rosenberg (see Fogel 2004a). This theory points to the existence of a synergism between technological and physiological improvements that has produced a form of human evolution that is biological but not genetic, rapid, culturally transmitted, and not necessarily stable. The process is still ongoing in both rich and developing countries.

Unlike the genetic theory of evolution through natural selection, which applies to the whole history of life on earth, technophysio evolution applies only to the last three hundred years of human history, and particularly to the last century.[4] The theory of technophysio evolution rests on the proposition that during the last three hundred years, particularly during the last century, human beings have gained an unprecedented degree of control over their environment – a degree of control so great that it sets them apart not only from all other species but also from all previous generations of *Homo sapiens*. This new degree of control has enabled *Homo sapiens* to increase its average body size by over 50 percent, to increase its average longevity by more than 100 percent, and to greatly improve the robustness and capacity of vital organ systems.[5]

Figure 5.1 helps to point up how dramatic the change in the control of the environment after 1700 has been. During its first two hundred thousand or so years, the population of *Homo sapiens* increased at an exceedingly slow rate. The discovery of agriculture about eleven thousand years ago broke the tight constraint on the food supply imposed by a hunting and gathering technology, making it possible to release between 10 and 20 percent of the labor force from the direct

---

[4] Fogel and Costa (1997) limit technophysio evolution to the last three hundred years for two reasons. It was not until about 1700 that changes in technology permitted population growth far in excess of previous rates. Moreover, after 1700, body weight and stature increased to unprecedented levels.

[5] Although a considerable body of empirical evidence has accumulated indicating that a "good" environment both speeds up biological development at young ages and delays the onset of chronic conditions at middle and late ages, there is as yet no agreed-on theory about the cellular and molecular processes that explain these observations.

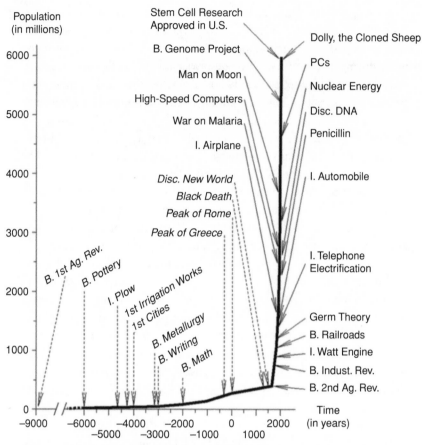

FIGURE 5.1. The growth of world population and some major events in the history of technology. *Note:* There is usually a lag between the invention (I) of a process or a machine and its general application to production. "Beginning" (B) usually means the earliest stage of the diffusion process. *Sources:* Derry and Williams (1960); Clark (1961); Piggott (1965); Trewartha (1969); McNeill (1971); Cipolla (1974); Fagan (1977). See also Slicher Van Bath (1963); Wrigley (1987); Allen (1992); Allen (1994).

production of food and also giving rise to the first cities. The new technology of food production was so superior to the old that it was possible to support a much higher rate of population increase than had existed prior to circa 9000 BCE. Yet, as Figure 5.1 shows, the advances in the technology of food production after the second agricultural revolution (which began about 1700 BCE) were far more dramatic than the earlier breakthrough because they permitted the population to increase at so high a rate that the line of population appears to explode, rising almost vertically. The new technological breakthroughs in manufacturing, transportation, trade, communications, energy production, leisure-time services, and medical services were in many respects even more striking than those in agriculture. Figure 5.1 emphasizes the huge acceleration in both population and technological change during the twentieth century. The increase in the world's population between 1900 and 1990 was four times as great as the increase during the whole previous history of humankind.

TECHNOPHYSIO EVOLUTION AND THE REDUCTION
IN INEQUALITY DURING THE TWENTIETH CENTURY

The twentieth century contrasts sharply with the record of the two preceding centuries. In every measure that we have bearing on the standard of living, such as real income, homelessness, life expectancy, and height, the gains of the lower classes have been far greater than those experienced by the population as a whole, whose overall standard of living has also improved.

The *Gini ratio*, which is also called the *concentration ratio*, is the measure of the inequality of the income distribution most widely used by economists.[6] This measure varies between 0 (perfect equality) and 1 (maximum inequality). In the case of England, for example, which has the longest series of income distributions, the Gini ratio stood at about 0.65 near the beginning of the eighteenth century, at about 0.55 near the beginning of the twentieth century, and at 0.32 in 1973, when it bottomed out, not only in Britain but also in the United States and other rich nations.[7] This measure indicates that over two-thirds of the reduction in the inequality of income distributions between 1700 and 1973 took place during the twentieth century. The large decrease in such inequality, coupled with the rapid increase in the average real income of the English population, means that the per capita income of

---

[6] Stature and Gini ratios are significantly correlated, but as the following discussion of height and BMI indicates, the anthropometric measures reveal important aspects of welfare that are not as apparent in the movement of Gini ratios.

[7] There has been a rise in the Gini ratio since 1973 in virtually all the rich nations for which such information is available (see Fogel 2000).

the lower classes was rising much more rapidly than the income of the middle or upper classes.[8]

A similar conclusion is implied by the data on life expectancies. For the cohort born about 1875, there was a gap of seventeen years between the average length of life of the British elite and of the population as a whole. There is still a social gap in life expectancies among the British, but today the advantage of the richest classes over the rest of the population is only about four years. Thus about three-quarters of the social gap in longevity has disappeared. As a consequence, the life expectancy of the lower classes increased from forty-one years at birth in 1875 to about seventy-four years today, while the life expectancy of the elite increased from fifty-eight years at birth to about seventy-eight years. If anything sets the twentieth century apart from the past, it is this huge increase in the longevity of the lower classes.[9]

Data on stature also indicate the high degree of inequality during the nineteenth century. At the close of the Napoleonic wars, a typical British male worker at maturity was about 5 inches shorter than a mature male of upper-class birth. There is still a gap in stature between the workers and the elite of Britain, but now the gap is only on the order of an inch. Height differentials by social class have virtually disappeared in Sweden and Norway but not yet in the United States. Statistical analysis across a wide array of rich and poor countries today shows a strong correlation between stature and the Gini ratio (Rona et al. 1978; Steckel 1995).

Weight is another important measure of inequality. Despite the great emphasis in recent years on weight reduction, the world still suffers more from undernutrition and underweight than from overweight, as the World Health Organization has repeatedly pointed out. Although one should not minimize the afflictions caused by overnutrition, it is important to recognize that even in rich countries such as the United States, undernutrition remains a significant problem, especially among impoverished pregnant women, children, and the aged.

---

[8] On trends in the Gini ratio between c. 1690 and 1973 and the debate over this trend, see Soltow (1968), Lindert and Williamson (1982), Williamson (1985), Feinstein (1988), and Floud et al. (1990).

[9] Data for males are presented in Case et al. (1962), Hollingsworth (1977), and Hattersley (1999).

The secular increase in body builds is due primarily to the great improvement in socioeconomic conditions over the past several centuries rather than to genetic factors, as can be seen by considering Holland. The average height of young adult males was only 64 inches in that country during the middle of the nineteenth century. The corresponding figure today is about 72 inches. An increase of 8 inches in just four generations cannot be due to natural selection or genetic drift because such processes require much longer time spans. Nor can it be attributed to heterosis (hybrid vigor) because Holland's population has remained relatively homogeneous and because the effects of heterosis in human populations have been shown both empirically and theoretically to have been quite small. It is hard to come up with credible explanations for the rapid increase in heights that do not turn on environmental factors, especially improvements in nutrition and health. These environmental factors appear to be still at work. Stature is still increasing, although at a somewhat slower rate, and nations have not yet reached a mean height that represents the biological limit of humankind under current biomedical technology (Van Wieringen 1986; Fogel 1992; Drukker 1994; Schmidt et al. 1995; Drukker and Tassenaar 1997).

Homelessness is another indicator of the dramatic reduction in inequality during the twentieth century. Down to the middle of the nineteenth century, between 10 and 20 percent of the population in Britain and on the Continent were homeless persons whom officials classified as vagrants and paupers. Estimates of vagrancy and pauper rates in the United States during the nineteenth century are less certain, but these rates appear to have reached European levels in the major cities during the middle decades of that century. When we speak of homelessness in the United States today, we are talking about rates below 0.4 percent of the population. Many of the homeless today are mentally ill individuals prematurely released from psychiatric institutions that are inadequately funded. Many others are chronically poor and inadequately trained for the current job market (Colquhoun 1814; Soltow 1968; Cipolla 1980; Lindert and Williamson 1982; Himmelfarb 1983; Hannon 1984a; Hannon 1984b; Laslett 1984; Hannon 1985; Fogel 1987; Fogel 1989; Fogel 1993; Jencks 1994).

The relatively generous poverty program developed in Britain during the second half of the eighteenth century and the bitter attacks on that program by Malthus and others have given the unwarranted impression that government transfers played a major role in the secular decline in beggary and homelessness. Despite the relative generosity of English poor relief between 1750 and 1834, beggary and homelessness fluctuated between 10 and 20 percent. Despite the substantial reduction in the proportion of national income transferred to the poor as a result of the poor laws of 1834 and later years, homelessness declined sharply during the late nineteenth and early twentieth centuries.

The fact is that government transfers were incapable of solving the problems of beggary and homelessness during the eighteenth and much of the nineteenth centuries because the root cause of the problems was chronic malnutrition. Even during the most generous phases of the relief program, the bottom fifth of the English population was so severely malnourished that it lacked the energy for adequate levels of work (Fogel 1997; Floud et al., forthcoming).

At the end of the eighteenth century, British agriculture, even when supplemented by imports, was simply not productive enough to provide more than 80 percent of the potential labor force with enough calories to sustain regular manual labor. It was the huge increases in English productivity during the later part of the nineteenth and the early twentieth centuries that made it possible to feed even the poor at relatively high caloric levels. Begging and homelessness were reduced to exceedingly low levels, by nineteenth-century standards, only when the bottom fifth of the population acquired enough calories to permit regular work. The principal way in which government policy contributed to that achievement was through its public health programs. By reducing exposure to disease, more of the calories that the poor ingested were made available for work.

## CONCLUSION

Technophysio evolution implies that some theoretical propositions that underlie some current economic models are misspecified because the initial endowments of health capital of successive cohorts increased over the course of the twentieth century. The common assumption that the endowment of human physiological capacity is fixed, so that medical intervention can only slow down the rate of deterioration in the original endowment, means that ways of forecasting future improvement in human physiology are sometimes neglected and that possible paths of increase in health endowments play little role in forecasting future health care costs or longevity.[10]

The theory of technophysio evolution implies that health endowments in a given population change with the year of birth. It also points to complex interactions between date of birth and the outcome of exposures to given risk factors. Hence not all improvements in the outcome of exposure to health risks between, say, 1970 and 1990 are due to health interventions during that period. Improvements in life expectancy may depend only partly on the more effective medical technologies of those years. It could also reflect the improved physiologies experienced by later birth cohorts that are due to improved technologies in food production, public health practices, personal hygiene, diets, and medical interventions put into place decades before 1970 and hence cannot be attributed exclusively, perhaps even primarily, to health inputs between 1970 and 1990. Moreover, many health interventions that are effective at late ages today would not be feasible if the level of physiological capital at late ages was as low today as it was at the beginning of the twentieth century.

---

[10]Among the exceptions are Rosenzweig and Schultz (1988) and Dasgupta (1993).

# 6

## Some Common Problems in Analysis
## and Measurement

This chapter discusses two common errors made by economists when dealing with issues of health, longevity, and equity: (1) measuring changes in crude death rates (CDR) over time by ratios rather than by differences and (2) measuring the income elasticity of the demand for food from cross-sectional rather than time series data. This chapter also discusses the merits of an analytical tool, Waaler surfaces, which brings height, weight, body mass index (BMI), and risks of mortality into a unified mathematical structure that is useful for estimating long-term trends.

### USING RATIOS OF CDR INSTEAD OF DIFFERENCES

Environmental conditions were far more severe in 1900 than in recent decades. There are many ways this can be measured, and one of them is by the infant death rate. Figure 6.1 presents some results of an ongoing study of changes in disparities in infant mortality during the twentieth century by the neighborhoods of the twenty-four largest U.S. cities in 1900. The study presently uses wards averaging about thirty thousand people as the unit of observation, but such large units tend to mask disparities since they often combine both rich and poor neighborhoods. In the future, it will be possible to conduct the analyses at the level of census districts, which average about eight thousand individuals and are more homogeneous with respect to socioeconomic status and health conditions than wards.

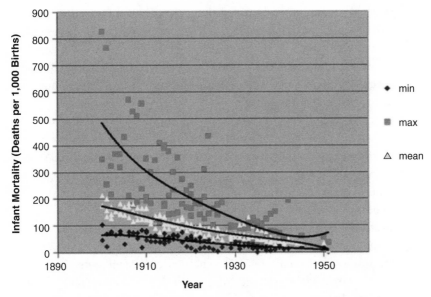

FIGURE 6.1. Preliminary findings on trends in disparities in infant death rates of the wards of ten U.S. cities, 1900–1950. *Source:* Center for Population Economics website (http://www.cpe.uchicago.edu/). This diagram shows that between 1900 and 1950, more than 80% of the difference in the infant mortality rate between the worst and best wards of ten large cities had disappeared.

However, even when the analysis is conducted at the ward level, the results are striking, as shown by Figure 6.1. In this figure, the $y$ axis is the infant death rate, and the $x$ axis is year. There are three sets of observations: the maximum infant death rates of wards in ten large cities are clustered around the top line; the minimum infant death rates are clustered around the bottom line; and the line in the middle represents the average.[1]

The main point of Figure 6.1 is how wide the range in infant death rates were at the beginning of the period: 246 per 1,000 between the best and the worst wards in 1900. However, by 1940, the differential between the best and the worst wards had declined to about 46 per 1,000. During the first four decades of the twentieth century, the spread between the best and the worst wards diminished by 81 percent.

---

[1] The cities observed are Baltimore, Boston, Milwaukee, New York, Newark, Philadelphia, St. Louis, Buffalo, Chicago, and Washington, D.C.

Hence the first point to be noted about changes and disparities in the twentieth century is that the range of differences in exposure to disease has narrowed greatly over the course of the century. The disparities we observe today are much smaller than they used to be. From the perspective of 1900, we are currently engaged in fine-tuning, not in gross corrections of disparities.

That is the result one gets when looking at differences in crude death rates. What happens if one looks at the ratio? The ratio of the crude death rates between the worst and best wards was 3.36 (350/104) in 1900, but in 1940, the ratio was 3.30 (66/20). Using ratios, it appears that there was no improvement in health disparities between 1900 and 1940 because the ratio of mortality in the worst wards to mortality in the best showed virtually no improvement. Which is the better measure of changes in disparities – changes in differences in CDR or changes in the ratios? The change in differences is consistent with the very large increase in life expectancy, the sharp decline in morbidity from a series of diseases that were deadly to infants, and the widespread improvement in housing and living standards generally.

Ratios give the wrong measure because of a mathematical artifact. When denominators are relatively small, a small change in the denominator can have a big effect on the value of the ratio. In the case of Figure 6.1, a modest improvement of conditions in the healthy wards obscures the huge improvement of conditions in the most unhealthy wards, when ratios are the measure of choice.

## ESTIMATING THE INCOME ELASTICITY OF FOOD CONSUMPTION FROM CROSS-SECTIONAL DATA

The explosion of population growth in the Third World after World War II led to fears of widespread food crises along Malthusian lines. It was thought that the production of food in poor countries could not keep up with population growth. The upward pressure on prices of lagging supply would cause already malnourished people to further reduce their consumption of food. There were also fears that the demand for food could grow more rapidly than population, putting further upward pressure on price. With estimates of the income elasticity of the demand for food ranging to above 0.8, the positive growth rates of gross domestic product in China, India, and other countries could, ironically, intensify the food crises. Although food shortages and famines did occur, the economic analyses were flawed because they were based on estimates of the income elasticities of the demand for food that were too high.

It is a common practice of economists to estimate such elasticities from cross-sectional surveys of household consumption. The practice is promoted by the availability of data because longitudinal studies of household consumption of food over the life cycle are rare. Indeed, life-cycle patterns of consumption are often inferred from cross-sectional differences by age. Some consumption studies are measured by the monetary outlays, others by the caloric value of purchased food. I focus on elasticity estimates based on calories, arguing that even these more modest estimates are much too high. A cross-sectional study of English working-class families in the eighteenth and nineteenth centuries produced elasticities in the neighborhood of 0.6 (Clark et al. 1995; Floud et al., 2011).

Can longitudinal estimates of the income elasticity of the demand for calories by individuals be inferred from cross-sectional studies of the relationship between income and calories? One way of getting at this issue is to consider the following identity:

$$C = B + M + W + A + L. \tag{1}$$

In illustrating the problems I have in mind, I will apply Equation (1) to data from household studies of English consumption during the late eighteenth century made famous in economics by an article by George Stigler (1954) and a fairly large number of subsequent studies of the same data sets by numerous economic historians.

The rate of change transformation of (1) is

$$\overset{*}{C} = \gamma_1 \overset{*}{B} + \gamma_2 \overset{*}{M} + \gamma_3 \overset{*}{W} + \gamma_4 \overset{*}{A} + \gamma_5 \overset{*}{L}, \tag{2}$$

where

$C$ = average daily kcal available (allotted, purchased) per consuming unit

$B$ = kcal required for the basal metabolic rate (BMR)

$M$ = additional kcal required for baseline maintenance

$A$ = kcal excreted in urine and feces (often called the Atwater factor when expressed as a share of kcal ingested)

$L$ = kcal produced but not ingested

$W$ = kcal required for work (which includes all discretionary activities requiring energy)

$\gamma_1$, $\gamma_2$, $\gamma_3$, $\gamma_4$, $\gamma_5$ = the shares of $B, M$, etc., in $C$

$*$ = the rate of change of a variable

My approximate estimates of $\gamma_i$ for England and Wales during the eighteenth and early nineteenth centuries are as follows:

$$\overset{*}{C} = 0.47\ \overset{*}{B} + 0.13\ \overset{*}{M} + 0.20\ \overset{*}{W} + 0.10\ \overset{*}{A} + 10\ \overset{*}{L}. \qquad (3)$$

The last two terms of (3) represent food that is wasted (not metabolized). If one considers only the distribution of energy that is metabolized, the three coefficients would be about 0.59, 0.16, and 0.25. Note that nutritional manuals take account of the current level of $A$ when reporting the caloric value of a unit of food. Hence $\gamma_4 A$ refers to the extra losses of ingested calories such as those incurred during eighteenth-century Britain.

Which variables in Equation (3) would be correlated with changes in current income (i.e., are endogenous during the period at issue)? That is the implicit question that is posed when one assumes that a cross-sectional regression of calories available for consumption on income provides an estimate of how caloric consumption will increase with the changes in real income over time.

Recent biomedical evidence indicates that the mechanisms controlling not only adult height but also adult weight (the determinants of $B$ and $M$) are to a considerable degree established in utero and during the first three years after birth. Barker (1998) reports that such measures as weight at birth and the ponderal index predict not only adult BMI but also the ratio of hip-to-waist circumferences (a measure of the distribution of body fat). Hence the variations in the income elasticity of $B$ and $M$ for particular individuals are constrained by the individuals' developmental history and are both quite low and, as a first approximation, could be put at zero.

The elasticity of $A$ with respect to current income is also very low as physiological studies indicate that $A$ depends on exposure to disease, the amount of nonstarch polysaccharides (dietary fiber) in the diet, and the absorptive capacity of the mucosal cells of the gastrointestinal tract, which is influenced by nutritional status. Nor would one expect $L$, losses of nutrients in cooking, spoilage, losses to rodents and other small animals, and plate waste, to be significantly correlated to changes in current income during the periods at issue.

The key point arising from Equations (1)–(3) is that cross-sectional regressions of calories on income reflect mainly the overwhelming influence of biological constraints, which are relatively fixed for particular individuals within a population at a point in time, although there is considerable variation in these physiological constraints from one person to another in that population. Consequently, what these cross-sectional regressions reflect primarily are differences in the levels of these constraints when individuals are grouped by income. They do not imply that mature individuals at low incomes who have low requirements for $B$ and $M$ will be able to alter these requirements at will by 50 or 100 percent merely by gaining income.

Although $B$ and $M$ are largely constrained over the lifetime of an individual (there is some variation over prime working ages), $B$ and $M$ have had a strong upward trend over time. In the case of French males aged eighteen to thirty years, for example, $B$ and $M$ have increased by about one-third between the early decades of the eighteenth century and 1990. Moreover, various factors (such as high rates of exposure to disease and impaired physiologies) that diminished the efficiency with which the body metabolized ingested nutrients have gradually been overcome (cf. Dasgupta 1993). Thus time series data yield much different, and generally much lower, estimates of the income elasticity of the demand for calories.

Table 6.1 shows income elasticities of the demand for calories calculated from time-series data for eight countries over periods varying from thirty-eight to two hundred years. All of these are well below the neighborhood of the 0.6 elasticity commonly calculated from cross-sectional data. Of the six elasticities computed from data for recent decades, the highest, 0.30, for the United States, is half the elasticity commonly computed from cross-sections. The elasticities computed for China, India, Germany, and Italy for recent decades vary between 0.20 and 0.26. The figure for Japan is much lower, just 0.07. Despite a quite rapid rise in average annual per capita income (4.2% per annum)

TABLE 6.1. *Income Elasticities of the Demand for Calories in Eight Nations (Computed from Time-Series Data)*

| Country | Time Period for Calculation | Elasticity |
| --- | --- | --- |
| 1. China | 1962–2000 | 0.26 |
| 2. India | 1961–2000 | 0.2 |
| 3. Japan | 1961–2000 | 0.07 |
| 4. Germany | 1961–2000 | 0.23 |
| 5. Italy | 1961–2000 | 0.21 |
| 6. United States | 1961–2000 | 0.3 |
| 7. France | 1807–2000 | 0.22 |
| 8. England/United Kingdom | 1800–2000 | 0.15 |

*Sources:* FAOSTAT; World Bank; Maddison (1991, 2001); Fogel (2004b).

during the last four decades of the twentieth century, the Japanese have resisted the temptation to raise their level of caloric intake as much as other rich countries have. This abstention from caloric gluttony coincides with the sharp increase in Japanese life expectancy between 1960 and 2002, about thirteen years, which is nearly twice the increase (seven years) experienced by the more gluttonous Americans (Keyfitz and Flieger 1990; Population Reference Bureau 2003).

For France and England, it is possible to compute income elasticities of the demand for calories over the last two centuries. These elasticities are relatively low, especially for England. England had a higher caloric intake in 1961 than France, Germany, or Italy, but while its neighbors increased caloric consumption substantially over the next four decades (by 26% in the case of Italy), England's consumption increased by only 2 percent. I shall probe this puzzle in the next section.

What are the possible biases embedded in Table 6.1? To examine this issue, I presume that the per capita demand curve for calories is log linear, as shown in Equation (4):

$$C = DY^{\gamma} P^{-e}. \qquad (4)$$

Differentiating Equation (4) totally and rearranging terms, we obtain Equation (5):

$$\gamma = \frac{\overset{*}{C}}{\overset{*}{Y}} + \frac{\varepsilon \overset{*}{P}}{\overset{*}{Y}} - \frac{\overset{*}{D}}{\overset{*}{Y}}, \qquad (5)$$

where

C = per capita demand for calories

D = a vector of variable that can shift the demand curve

Y = per capita income

P = price of calories

$\gamma$ = income elasticity of the demand for calories

$\varepsilon$ = price elasticity of the demand for calories

* = the rate of change of a variable

It follows from Equation (5) that failure to take account of the very substantial and largely steady secular decline in the price of calories biases the estimate of $\gamma$ upward. Neglect of a number of the other variables represented in D also biases upward the estimates of $\gamma$ in Table 6.1. These include improvement in the thermodynamic efficiency of the body due to improvement in physiological capital, such as increased efficiency of mucosal cells; reduced episodes of infectious diseases that inhibit caloric metabolism; and a reduced proportion of fiber in the diet. Because each of these variables is the equivalent of a reduction in the price of calories, the effect of these variables in Equation (5) is to reduce the value of $\gamma$, and neglect of them in the calculation of Table 6.1 imparted an upward bias.

Changes in lifestyle are a more difficult issue. Whether the level of energy-requiring activities has gone up or down is not entirely clear. There has been a significant change in the composition of energy-using activities. Even if the shift has been away from high-energy-using activities (measured as a multiple of BMR), that fact that individuals are on average heavier than they used to be may increase the total demand for energy.

## USE OF BMI CURVES TO IDENTIFY OPTIMAL LEVELS OF WEIGHT (ADJUSTED FOR HEIGHT) INSTEAD OF WEIGHT BY HEIGHT SURFACES

The U-shaped BMI risk curves, brought to the attention of biodemographers by Waaler in 1984, have become a staple in the analysis of health risks owing to over- and underweight (adjusted for height).

Such curves, which have now been estimated for many places and time periods, generally are quite flat between BMIs of 21 and 27. However, risks rise quite sharply at BMIs less than 20 or more than 27. Men are at greater risk than women at high BMIs, but women are at greater risk than men at low BMIs.

Although BMI risk curves are revealing, they are not sufficient to shed light on the debate over whether moderate stunting impairs health when weight-for-height is adequate. To get at the small-but-healthy issue, one needs an isomortality surface that relates the risk of death to height and weight simultaneously. Such a surface, presented in Figure 6.2, combines three different types of curves. The solid elliptical curves are isomortality risk curves, each of which traces out all the combinations of height and weight that represent a given level of risk. Transecting the isomortality map is a set of iso-BMI curves, represented by dashed lines. Each iso-BMI curve is the locus of all of the combinations of height and weight that yield a specific level of BMI, ranging from 16 to 34. The bold curve running through the minimum point of each isomortality curve gives the weight that minimizes risk at each height.

Figure 6.2 shows that even when body weight is maintained at an ideal level (BMI = 25), short men are at substantially greater risk of death than tall men. Figure 6.2 also shows that the ideal BMI varies with height. A BMI of 25 is ideal for men in the neighborhood of 176 cm (69 inches), but for tall men, the ideal BMI is between 22 and 24, while for short men (under 168 cm or 66 inches), the ideal BMI is about 26.

A number of recent studies suggest that current mean body builds, even in countries abundant in calories, still appear to be suboptimal when the optimal height and BMI are defined as those that minimize the age-specific odds of dying or of developing chronic diseases over a specific interval. Moreover, trends in nutritional status and risk vary significantly even among rich countries. This point is illustrated by Figure 6.2.

Superimposed on the Waaler surface in Figure 6.2 are rough estimates of the average heights and weights in both France and England at several dates between 1705 and 2001. In 1705 the French were not only much shorter but their BMIs were much lower than those of the English. During the nineteenth century, the French caught up with,

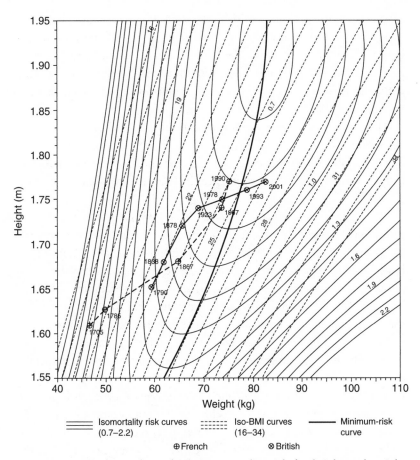

FIGURE 6.2. Waaler surface of relative mortality risk for height and weight among Norwegian males aged fifty to sixty-four with a plot of the estimated French and English heights and weights since 1705 at ages twenty-five to thirty-nine.

and, by 1867, exceeded the English in BMI. However, they remained several centimeters shorter than the English. Between 1867 and 1967, French stature remained below that of the English, but the gap narrowed and the French achieved higher BMIs. Still, down to the mid-twentieth century, the English advantage in height more than offset the French advantage in BMI with respect to the risk of death. After 1967, French stature increased quite rapidly, and its BMI moved closer to the optimal level, mainly because at taller heights, lower BMIs are optimal.

During the same period, English gains in stature were modest, but their BMI increased so rapidly that by 2001, they were well in excess of the optimal level for their height. As a consequence, by the 1990s, English mortality risk associated with body builds exceeded that of the French. Although their statures were equal, the English were at a disadvantage because their BMI shot past the optimal level.

Thus Figure 6.2 illustrates how technophysio evolution conquered the severe malnutrition of past centuries. But in so doing, it created a new problem: overnutrition. Food has become so cheap that corpulence is no longer a sign of opulence; instead, it is a sign of weakness of will.

Have Waaler curves and surfaces been changing over time? It is too soon to answer that question with any confidence. Preliminary estimates of Waaler curves and surfaces for morbidity and mortality have been constructed from data obtained on Union Army veterans covering the period between 1890 and 1930. These preliminary studies indicate that the curve in BMI and mortality and the Waaler surface for these men are quite similar to that shown for Norwegian males.

Figure 6.2 implies that the cost of adaptation to inadequate food supplies by wasted and stunted individuals cannot be measured merely by using cross-sectional data to determine whether productivity is positively correlated with stature. Such cross-sectional procedures do not take into account the rate of decline in human capital over the life cycle. Since stunting accelerates the rate of depreciation in human capital over the life cycle, the discounted present value of output is, on average, lower than inferred from cross-sections. Even if, at a given age, a short person who is still in the labor force is as productive as a tall one, more short than tall persons of that age have left the labor force because of disability or death. Hence there is sample-selection bias in econometric studies that omit from consideration those members of a cohort who are no longer in the labor force. Even studies that show a positive effect of stature or BMI on output have biased the effect downward, unless they have taken account of the omitted observations.

Figure 6.3 calls attention to another problem that is often overlooked. To equalize the rate of depreciation in human capital, stunted individuals require higher BMIs than tall individuals. Earlier, it was noted that to equalize the odds of retaining good health in middle age, a male of 165 cm needs a BMI that is substantially higher than that

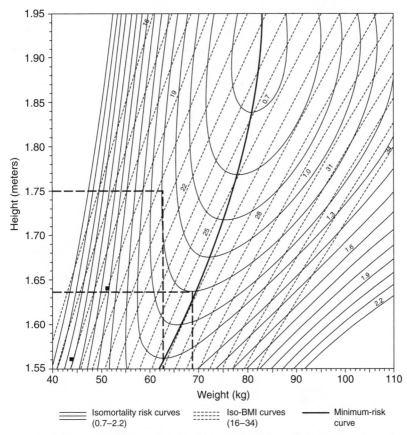

FIGURE 6.3. Isomortality curves of relative risk of dying for height and weight among Norwegian males aged fifty to sixty-four, with two plots.

required by a male of 181 cm. However, when risks are equalized (i.e., when two or more sets of height and weight points lie on the same isomortality curve), the BMR of the stunted individual is higher than that of the tall individual. Figure 6.3 demonstrates that saving on the energy for basal metabolism requires an increased rate of depreciation in human capital. Hence the essence of adaptation via body size to an inadequate food supply is a trade-off of current metabolic needs for an increased life-cycle risk of morbidity and mortality. Indeed, in the case illustrated in Figure 6.3, a long-run (over several decades) adaptation to a reduction in the food supply through a 5 percent reduction in stature and BMI requires a 19 percent increase in the risk of dying. In the short run, adaptation can only occur in weight (height remaining constant). The necessary weight reduction would be about 14 percent, and the risk of mortality would rise by 35 percent. Hence short-run adaptations are riskier than those that occur in the long run because of the distortion in body proportions.

As a Chicago economist, I cannot resist pointing out that in adaptation through stunting or wasting, as in so many other circumstances, there is no such thing as a free lunch.

# 7

## Afterword

### A Conversation with the Author

**Professor Fogel, welcome to Berkeley.**
Wonderful to be here.

**Where were you born and raised?**
I was born and raised in the Bronx – New York City, for Californians who may not have heard of the Bronx.

**That's right, although there are many émigrés here, so some of us have heard. In looking back, how do you think your parents shaped your thinking about the world?**
My parents were very loving, very optimistic people, and they gave me an optimistic outlook on life. My father arrived at Ellis Island penniless in 1922, and by 1929, he had saved enough money to open his first business. By 1939, even though the Great Depression was still in progress, he owned a business that employed over a hundred people.

I'll tell you something that reflected the improvement in the status of the Fogel family. My brother, who was six years older than me, and nine years ahead of me in school, was a freshman at City College in New York in 1936 when I was only ten years old. And I remember he and several of his friends having a conversation at my house one night when I was supposed to be asleep. The topic was what do you do for a date if you only have ten cents? The answer was, find a girl

The author was interviewed by Harry Kreisler of the University of California, Berkeley on November 16, 2004.

who is babysitting; a nickel will get you there and a nickel will bring you back. But by the time I went to college in 1944, it was at Cornell, a private school, and on an allowance that would have staggered my brother in 1936.

**And you were at Cornell during what years?**
From 1944 to 1948.

**Did your father want his sons to go into his business?**
Oh, he was very eager. One of the big disappointments in his life was that neither my brother nor I wanted to take over the business, and he eventually sold the business when he retired. So he was quite disappointed.

**Is there a common element in what drew you and your brother to university life?**
I was heavily influenced by my brother. He was my hero, and I wanted to emulate him when I was growing up. He was an extremely successful student. He was at the top of his high school class. He did very well in academic life, first in high school and then in college, and he inspired me by his achievements. He taught in the English department at Cornell University from 1949 until his retirement in 1990.

**How do you think the times affected you? You were probably too young to appreciate the Depression, but that's an era in which there's a lot of turbulence. Did that seep into your conscience? Not necessarily why you chose the academy, but the issues you would look at?**
Although I lived through the Depression, I thought it was a golden age, because my family life was so secure. I also had wonderful teachers – teachers who despite the Depression had optimistic outlooks. I remember in third or fourth grade a teacher saying that in the United States, anyone could be president. So I grew up with the belief that I could be president, too. I had the notion that there was a lot of opportunity, both from my parents and from my teachers.

**Before you went to college or in the beginning of college, you thought about being a scientist, right?**
Yes. I went to Stuyvesant High School, which was one of three science high schools in New York City, and my passion was physical chemistry. I wanted to go to Cal Tech to study with a man who had won the

Nobel Prize for physical chemistry some years earlier. But my mother wouldn't hear of my going to a college that was three thousand miles away from home. She wanted me to go to Columbia. My brother, whom I've described in print as "the great compromiser," proposed Cornell. I'd be away from home but still within a day's train ride of the city.

**So physical chemistry's loss was economics' gain. What drew you to economics?**
What drew me to economics was the great concern in Congress, the media, and among my teachers that the high unemployment levels of the Great Depression would return. There were also debates about whether the government might be able to prevent a depression by using Keynesian proposals. These debates were challenging, and I wanted to know more about these economic problems and what could be done about them.

**A second part of the story of your career and your work is that you are also a historian, and you bring history and economics together in your work. Help us understand how that came about. What made you bring history along in the work that you did in economics?**
I liked history. I used to read history for fun. I had very good history teachers in junior high school and high school, who made it a lively and living field. Then I had the good fortune that my principal teachers, both at the master's degree level and at the PhD level, were very historically oriented, particularly Simon Kuznets, who supervised my dissertation and was the third winner of the Nobel Prize in Economics.

**Did these teachers have a European background in their sense of history? Because one could say that Americans generally don't have as much of a sense of history.**
Simon Kuznets, who was born in Russia and came here at about age twenty, got a master's and then a PhD at Columbia University in the late 1920s and worked with Wesley Clair Mitchell, the founder of the National Bureau of Economic Research, who had a very strong historical orientation to economics. The National Bureau, in general, has appreciated history as a source of evidence and as a basis for forecasting likely developments in the economy. So I was with teachers who, although they were economists, valued history as a basis for forecasting.

**Tell us a little about the synergy between history and economics, because when one thinks of economics, one thinks of theory, but you often don't associate history with theory. There must be an interesting play that has helped you in your work.**

I was also very theoretically oriented. Again, I had very good theory teachers at Columbia, one of whom was George Stigler, another Nobel Prize winner. He was the first holder of the chair that I now hold. He was a mentor as well as a teacher when I came to Chicago as a young faculty member; he took an interest in me. He was very pleased to see how I was combining economic history with theory and helped to encourage me to develop that approach at the University of Chicago.

**You wrote that "the historical point of view makes you more aware of the evidence you need." Explain that to us.**

If you look at the kinds of problems we're now worried about – "we" being the Congress, the president, and other makers of national economic policy – we worry about the fact that the Social Security system may go bankrupt in thirty years, or that Medicare may go bankrupt in an even shorter time span. Well, if you're going to forecast thirty years in advance, are you just going to do it with today's data, or do you want to see how the demand for health care and the costs of providing it have changed over a substantial period in the past in order to forecast likely trends? You have to be a historian to be a good forecaster. You have to know what data to look at. Most of our forecasters, even though they're not trained as economic historians, have to learn a lot of economic history.

**Using the example of Social Security, then, it probably becomes important to understand how it came into being and what assumptions were built into the program, which have now changed as our historical situation has changed.**

Right. You need to go back into the history in order to know why we have, let's say, the kind of problems we have. That is, what was the outlook of the people who designed Social Security in the 1930s, and then redesigned it under the Great Society program? Their vision, the vision of the people who were trying to set up a system that would last for a while, provides a basis for thinking about what our problems are going to be in the future and how we can improve on the current design in order to avoid a crisis in the not-too-distant future.

**Part of the issue is financing, right? The way they chose to finance the system.**

Right, financing is the central issue. It's not that we're too poor a country. Today, we spend about 16 percent of our national income on health care. My forecast is that by 2040, we'll be spending about 29 percent – and there are some forecasters who think that health costs may rise to nearly a third of GDP. But if you go back to 1929, we only spent 3 percent of GDP. Today we are much healthier than we were in 1929, but we spend more than five times what was spent then.

The demand for health care is driven, not by the fact that we're getting more unhealthy, but by the fact that we're getting richer. Indeed, now we're so rich that we need to use only a small fraction of our income for what used to be thought of as the basic necessities of life – food, clothing, and shelter. At the beginning of the twentieth century, 75 percent of all household expenditures went for such necessities, and now it's less than a third.

And we're eating too much. We're eating more food and also more expensive food. A lot of what we call food is actually services, because food is now substantially prepared. Most of us have big freezers and a lot of our food is frozen. But even if you buy fresh food from the grocery store, say, spinach, it's prewashed. In my mother's day, if you bought spinach, the grocer would pick up a bunch of fresh spinach that was one-third sand by weight, wrap it in a newspaper, and my mother spent hours trying to wash the sand out. And even then, the spinach she gave me was a little on the gritty side. So now we eat a wider variety of foods, and these foods are relatively more expensive. We don't eat many grains anymore. We used to get 75 percent of our calories from grains. And yet, despite all of the improvements, food, clothing, and shelter account for just a third of all of our expenditures.

So we have a lot of other things to spend our income on. We spend some on education, and we spend some on health care. We also spend it on early retirement, compared to the beginning of the century. And we spend it on a variety of leisure-time activities.

**I hear you saying that history allows you to see the broad institutional context in which the Social Security program originally emerged, and**

history helps you see its evolution over time to where we are, and then
to project it in the future.

Right. And also how the society that the program is supposed to serve
has changed, how societal needs and interests have changed. So the
situation of old people at the time of Roosevelt was very different.

**What is your comment on the way this kind of analysis, which gives
us a sense of the whole picture over time, is then used by the people
who make policy? Do politicians still tend to get it wrong once they
have all of this information?**

I have a very high regard for the people in Congress who specialize in
these issues. They are very knowledgeable. They have excellent staffs,
and they invite academics to evaluate their proposals and approaches.
So I think Congress is very serious. It wants to do a good job on these
things. But jockeying elections distorts debate over the issues. The
party out of power emphasizes the failure of policy, while the party
in power emphasizes the achievements. But leaving aside what you
might call the theatrics of elections, I think politicians are generally
very well-informed, serious people who want to make sure that the
government serves the population well.

**Another important element of your work is the methodological sophis-
tication that you have brought to these studies. You were an early user
of computers to gather this information. You said in your lecture that
if the technology hadn't come in to assist you, the costs would have
been so prohibitive that you never could have done some of the work,
for example, on aging. Talk a little about that. You've made clear to
us the way you've brought history and economic theory to the agenda,
but also the sophisticated instruments that you had to work with were
very important.**

We've been studying the aging of the Union Army cohort, the cohort
that fought during the Civil War. That was the first cohort to reach
age sixty-five in the twentieth century. So if we're interested in how
the process of aging has changed during living memory, that's an
important cohort to study.

**And there are data. The War Department gathered the information
about these people.**

Yes. The nature of the Union Army pension was such that the average pensioner had a full-scale physical examination about once every three years. Those medical records have survived in the National Archives. Our research team is 50 percent physicians, and they've gone over these records. They said that if they were in a rural area and without access to the high-tech diagnostic techniques we use today, they could not have done better than these doctors did. So it was absolutely first-rate clinical medicine.

These records have enabled us to learn a great deal about differences in the burden of diseases and in the process of aging over three cohorts. The Union Army cohort aged about ten years more rapidly than we do. For example, in my cohort, the average age of onset of arthritis is about age sixty-five. In the Union Army cohort, it was about age fifty-four. So we pushed back the age of onset of arthritis by eleven years. The same thing is true of heart disease, respiratory disease, and so on. All these things start later. Not only that, the proportion whoever get these diseases is about a third less than it used to be. And once you develop a chronic condition, we have excellent interventions. We have drug interventions and other surgical interventions that are effective. Even when these interventions do not extend our life, they improve the quality of life.

**Let's talk a little about the work you've done on aging. Bringing these data to bear on the questions you're interested in about aging, what did you conclude about the causes of the differences in the onset of these chronic illnesses?**
We concluded that we should apply for another grant! And we have. So we're still working on it.

We have some conclusions, but most of the research is ahead of us. I spoke about some of the findings in my first Hitchcock Lecture. We believe that the principal explanation for the increase in life expectancy and the reduction in disabilities during the course of the twentieth century is the cleaning up of the environment. Our evidence indicates that the exposure to severe "health insults" (to use an epidemiologist's word) during developmental ages did long-term damage to the physiology of the people who were exposed to them.

**This is at birth? Or in the early stages in life?**

It includes in utero, but it's throughout the life cycle. The years of early life are the most sensitive years when organs are still developing. Even if no new cells are being added, the cells are getting bigger. That's why we get bigger. In some organ systems, such as the central nervous system, new cells keep getting added throughout the developmental ages. That means if you have processes that interfere with cellular formation, you may have deficits in the organs that are not immediately apparent but take the form of earlier breakdown at middle and late ages. There have been a number of studies in the United States and several countries in Europe, and in India, among others, that reveal a high correlation between characteristics of the fetus at birth and characteristics of development during the first year of life that predict such things as the odds of having high blood pressure or type II diabetes or chronic respiratory disease in your fifties and sixties.

**Is one preliminary conclusion that health expenditures devoted to early child care could be an important way to address some of these problems?**

Yes, that's a definite policy implication that's arisen from this work. Not just early child care, but prenatal care as well. The prenatal period and early childhood period, investments in good health, including counseling of mothers – getting women who smoke to stop smoking, getting women who drink to stop drinking during pregnancy, and to eat appropriately. All those things will lead to healthier fetuses, and healthier infants, and healthier life throughout the developmental ages and into middle and old age.

**Your work transcends economics and history. It's quite interdisciplinary in terms of all the fields of knowledge that come to bear in reaching these kinds of conclusions.**

That's right. I spend more of my time these days with doctors than I do with economists. Although, don't get me wrong, I love economics.

**That's good! You use a term in your lecture and in your book, the theory of *technophysio evolution*. Talk a little about that, because it points to the insights that are coming from all these different fields about what has created the conditions for this change in people's health.**

One of the things that we've done in our search for evidence bearing on the explanation for the enormous increase in life expectancy over the past three centuries has been to identify physiological changes that may have explanatory power. In this connection, one of the most important measures is a class of measures called anthropometric measures. They're physical characteristics of the body such as height, sitting height, the amount of fat that you have on your body, and a measure called the body mass index, which is weight standardized for height.

Improvement in these anthropometric measures has been shown to be highly correlated with the increase in life expectancy and the reduction in morbidity over time and over the life cycle. A person born in 1950 has more than 2.5 times the life expectancy of someone who was born in 1700. So over three hundred years, we've more than doubled life expectancy, we've increased average weight by 50 percent, and we've added nearly a foot to stature. What goes along with the difference in these external measures are stronger lungs, stronger hearts, improved respiration, stronger electrical signals across membranes – so, in every respect that we've been able to measure with high-tech procedures, we are much better off physiologically. Unfortunately, there are still people who are as badly off in physiology because of malnutrition and exposure to disease in very poor countries as the French were before the French Revolution.

**I'm curious as I listen to you talk. Clearly methodology is important, history is important, economic theory is important. Over the lifetime of your career, you've addressed big projects – slavery, railroads, aging – and have tried to locate them and understand what these phenomena were in a broader institutional framework. What drew you to these subjects? Is it something in your background? Is it the evidence that's available? Just what interests you? I would be interested in the origins of the topics that you've selected.**
A lot of them are accidental, but the general trend is not accidental. When I was sitting in Simon Kuznets' class on economic development across countries and over time, at one point he said, "One of the most important factors in economic growth and development was the invention of the railroad, but no one has really studied it," and I said, "Oh, I like railroads." Actually, I had done my master's thesis on the Union Pacific Railroad, so I already knew something about it. So

I decided to write my PhD dissertation on railroads and American economic growth.

I got into the study of slavery as an accident. The precipitating factor in this case was the editing of a book called *The Reinterpretation of American Economic History*, which was supposed to bring together about thirty of the best articles in cliometrics, that is, in works of economic history using pretty high-tech statistics and econometrics. We divided the book into nine sections, one of which was on the economics of slavery. Stan Engerman and I wrote a long introduction to that section.

The work up until that day had focused on whether slavery was profitable or not and whether the slave South was growing more or less rapidly than the North. In the introduction, we asked, "What issues about slavery should the cliometricians take on next?" We said, "They ought to show how much less efficient slavery was than free agriculture." To emphasize that theme, we thought we would do a little back-of-the-envelope calculation. We thought that the back-of-the-envelope calculation would show that slavery was at least 50 percent less efficient, but when we did it, it turned out that the slave South was 6 percent more efficient than the free North. We were startled. We said, "Boy, we really messed that one up," and we started looking at it in a little bit more detail, and we redid the computation more carefully. At that point, we hoped that the South was at least a little less efficient. We thought maybe people had been too sanguine in thinking that there was a 50 percent difference. But when we redid the computation, the South turned out to be 36 percent more efficient than the North!

So at that stage, we applied for and received a large NSF grant to study slavery. One of the things we had to study was the demography of slavery, because the health and longevity of slaves were a factor in how you measured productivity. It was there that we got interested in differential mortality trends, and we began to realize that we knew very little about trends in mortality in the United States before the 1890s. We were aware that the Mormons had collected genealogical data that were available in Salt Lake City. With genealogical data, one could reconstruct the pattern of change in mortality. So we began a project on the improvements in American life expectancy from about 1710 on.

Such a project could not have been contemplated before the age of high-speed computers, which were generally not available in the 1950s. Those computers enabled us to get data that we knew were there but nobody previously thought were usable. With the appearance of high-speed mainframe computers, and later on, laptops that we could actually take in the archives, it became possible to input and process data at relatively low cost. We received in 1991 a grant to begin the study of the aging process in the Union Army. It was a three million dollar grant, and we calculated what it would have cost us to have done that project with the technology of 1978: the answer was about three hundred million dollars. We would have needed a special bill through Congress. It was way outside the parameters of even big social science grants at the National Science Foundation or the National Institutes of Health.

So the change in data-processing technology made it possible to engage in massive data retrieval. In the case of the Union Army sample, in order to get a picture of the changes in health over the life of a recruit, from early childhood to death, we had to link together information from twenty different data sources. To describe that life-cycle pattern, including all of the health information, takes fifteen thousand variables. When I was using computers in the mid- to late 1970s, five thousand observations, with maybe fifty variables on each observation, was thought to be the outer limit of what you could handle. Here we had forty thousand observations, with fifteen thousand variables on each observation. So we had to input and manage six hundred million pieces of information, which was way beyond the limits of existing software. And I won't say that solving these problems was a snap, but it was doable.

**So the long-term trend is that one problem leads you to another, and the technology coming on board allows you to do things you could not have done in the first instance.**

At every stage in our work on long-term changes in health and longevity, we were pushing the limits of technology, and our main problem was to convince our peers that it could be done. They were all convinced that the topic was a good idea, but they had to be convinced that the project could actually be implemented, and implemented within the expenditure limits that we were proposing.

I guess some of these results, like the results on slavery, were pretty controversial. So it's a combination of what the evidence shows, on the one hand, being controversial, but also the controversy aroused by saying, "We want to go in this direction."

It was very controversial even within our own research group. There were times when I thought that Stan was nuts, and there were times that he thought that I was nuts, and our graduate research assistants sometimes thought we were both nuts, although sometimes they were ahead of us. But our findings on slavery were so contrary to received wisdom.

On slavery.

On slavery. When we got our first results, we were so dubious about them that we delayed publication for two years, trying to falsify the result. We only published it after two years, when we couldn't break our own findings.

When one thinks of creativity or of the work of Nobel laureates, one thinks of that eureka moment, where suddenly things are put together. Is that what you've experienced in your career, or is it more the initial choices about directions that you want to go that are really more important? What is the best description of the most exciting moments in your career?

Well, there are a lot of eureka moments, but it's not, "Eureka! I found it!" It's "Eureka! It's just the opposite from the way we all thought it would be!"

If you take the slavery project, some of the most important turning points were discoveries by our graduate students that we never dreamed of. They would give us a result, and I would say, "That can't be true. You must have done something wrong." I only gradually realized that it was my priors that were wrong; their work was right. So we got started on tracks that we never anticipated. It was very collective. It was the work of a research group, not a lonely scholar with the light suddenly coming on. It was collective research. It took a lot of labor. It took a lot of different skills. Nobody has all those skills – programming skills, analytical skills, historical skills, statistical skills. Different people contributed different kinds of expertise, and they all functioned as part of a research program. I don't know of anyone who participated in our research groups who at the end of it could say, "Gee, I knew that at the beginning."

How would you characterize the people who do well in the kind of work we're talking about? Are there particular skills or characteristics that are good to have?
Hard work.

**Hard work. Patience?**
Hard work, patience, willingness to put up with tedium. At the end, something interesting might come out of it, but in order to get to that interesting or surprising thing, there's a lot of tedium you have to overcome.

**If students were to watch this interview, how would you advise them to prepare for the future in the kinds of fields that you work in?**
Just study the basic disciplines. If you're in economics, get the main foundations of economics, the theoretical, the statistical, and the empirical skills that we train PhD economists in. If you're a historian, learn the history of the period very thoroughly. Take advantage of quantitative data that may be available. It's not the only form of evidence, but it is an important additional form. Everyone now uses word processors and laptops, so the computer isn't as frightening as it was thirty years ago, when it seemed like some mysterious black box. Many students of history have picked up the skills that you need, let's say, to do a study in demographic history, or of changes in voting behavior in political history, or changes in the standard of living of the lower classes. Those skills are now widely available, and there are many people in history departments who have those skills and can convey it to their students.

**I infer from your writings, a small portion of which I've read, that you think writing is also important, clear writing.**
Writing is probably the single most important skill: the ability to communicate. That's what writing is. Some fields are so technical that the writing consists of a series of equations that can go on one page, and the only words are, "we begin with theorem one, then lemma one, lemma two, lemma three." All that goes in between these words is in Greek, and then at the end you say, q.e.d., that's it.

So there are fields of mathematics where you don't have to write well, although many of my friends in mathematics are more skilled in humane discipline than, let's say, social scientists are. So people in the sciences and in mathematics are very broad, humane, and with social scientific interests. That, I think, is part of American scientific culture.

**One final question: building on all that you study, where do you think the interesting problems are going to be in this cross between history and economics?**
I'm so focused on the economics and biodemography of aging that I'm not a good person to ask that question to, broadly. I do not follow economic history in the way that I once did. I still have a lot of friends in economic history, and I speak to them. So every few months they bring me up to date on something that's exciting and new. But I can tell you a lot about what's interesting in aging research.

**Please do.**
The central problem that needs to be answered is, will we be able to constrain the increase in the demand for health care? A related question is, what will the likely pattern of age-specific morbidity and disability rates be over the next several decades?

There is general agreement that for most conditions, they're going to become milder, pushed off further in time in terms of onset, but not necessarily in all conditions. There is some evidence that the prevalence of diabetes is increasing, and for younger people, there have been some increases in asthma. So within the framework of a general improvement in health, there can be reverses. Indeed, everything can be reversed, because these are not genetic changes, they're environmental changes. So a worsening of the environment for any one of a variety of reasons can cause serious setbacks.

As I said, I'm an optimist. I'm an optimist from early childhood on, and I believe that we're going to get healthier. In the book that I just published, I forecast that life expectancy during the current century will increase by another thirty years. So people who are undergraduates here will probably have an average length of life of about one hundred years.

**Well, on that very positive note, I want to thank you, Professor Fogel, for coming to Berkeley to give the Hitchcock Lectures and for taking the time to be on the show. Thank you very much.**
Thank you for inviting me.

# References

Abel W. 1980. *Agricultural Fluctuations in Europe from the Thirteenth to the Twentieth Centuries.* New York: St. Martin's Press.

Allen RC. 1992. *Enclosure and the Yeoman: The Agricultural Development of the South Midlands.* Oxford: Clarendon Press.

Allen R. 1994. Agriculture during the industrial revolution. In *The Economic History of Britain since 1700,* ed. Floud R, McCloskey D. Cambridge: Cambridge University Press.

Appleby A. 1978. *Famine in Tudor and Stuart England.* Stanford, CA: Stanford University Press.

Appleby A. 1979. Grain prices and subsistence crises in England and France, 1590–1740. *Journal of Economic History* 39: 865–867.

Bairoch P. 1973. Agriculture and the Industrial Revolution 1700–1914. In *The Fontana Economic History of Europe: The Industrial Revolution,* ed. Cipolla C. London: Collins.

Barker DJP. 1998. *Mothers, Babies, and Health in Later Life.* Edinburgh: Churchill Livingstone.

Barnes D. 1930. *A History of the English Corn Laws from 1660 to 1846.* London: Routledge.

Baxter J. 1875. *Statistics, Medical and Anthropological, of the Provost-Marshall-General's Bureau, Derived from Records of the Examination for Military Service in the Armies of the United States during the Late War of the Rebellion of over a Million Recruits, Drafted Men, Substitutes, and Enrolled men.* Washington, DC: Government Printing Office.

Bell F, Wade A, et al. 1992. *Life Tables for the United States Security Area 1900–2080.* Publication 11-11536. Washington, DC: Social Security Administration.

Bernard R.-J. [1969] 1975. Peasant diet in eighteenth-century Gevaudan. In *European Diet from Pre-Industrial to Modern Times,* ed. Forster E, Forster R. New York: Harper and Row.

147

Birchenall J. 2003. Airborne diseases: Tuberculosis in the Union Army. Presented at Joint Meeting of the Early Indicators of Later Work Levels, Disease and Death Program Project and Cohort Studies Groups, National Bureau of Economics, Cambridge, MA, April 25–26.

Blum J. 1978. *The End of the Old Order in Rural Europe*. Princeton, NJ: Princeton University Press.

Bongaarts J. 1980. Does malnutrition affect fecundity? A summary of the evidence. *Science* 208: 564–569.

Bourgeois-Pichat J. 1965. The general development of the population of France since the eighteenth century. In *Population in History: Essays in Historical Demography*, ed. Glass D, Eversley D. Chicago: Aldine.

Bowden P. 1967. Statistical appendix. In *The Agrarian History of England and Wales*, ed. Finberg H, Thirsk J. Cambridge: Cambridge University Press.

Bowden P. 1985. Appendix III, statistics. In *The Agrarian History of England and Wales*, vol. VII, ed. Thirsk J. Cambridge: Cambridge University Press.

Bridges T. 2002. Preliminary findings on the linkage between infant mortality and education during early 20th-century Chicago. Working paper, Center for Population Economics, University of Chicago.

British Association for the Advancement of Science. 1884. *Final Report of the Anthropometric Committee*. London.

Burnett J. 1979. *Plenty and Want*. London: Scholar Press.

Case R, et al. 1962. *Chester Beatty Research Institute Abridged Serial Life Tables, England and Wales 1841–1960, Part 1*. London: Chester Beatty Research Institute.

Cavalli-Sforza L, Bodmer W. 1971. *The Genetics of Human Populations*. San Francisco: W. H. Freeman.

Cavelaars A, Kunst A, et al. 2000. Persistent variation in average height between countries and between socio-economic groups: An overview of 10 European countries. *Annals of Human Biology* 27: 407–421.

Chamla M. 1983. L'evolution récente de la stature en Europe occidentale (periode 1960–1980). *Bulletin ed Memoire de la Societé d'Anthropologie de Paris* 10: 195–224.

Chandra R. 1975. Antibody formation in first and second generation offspring of nutritionally deprived rats. *Science* 4211: 289–290.

Chartres J. 1985. The marketing of agricultural produce. In *The Agrarian History of England and Wales*, volume VII, ed. Thirsk J. Cambridge: Cambridge University Press.

Chávez A, Martínez C, et al. 1995. The effect of malnutrition on human development: A 24-year study of well-nourished children living in a poor Mexican village. In *Community Based Longitudinal Studies of the Impact of Early Malnutrition on Child Health and Development: Classical Examples from Guatemala, Haiti and Mexico*, ed. Scrimshaw N. Boston: International Foundation for Developing Countries.

Cipolla C. 1974. *The Economic History of World Population*. Harmondsworth, UK: Penguin.

Cipolla C. 1980. *Before the Industrial Revolution: European Society and Economy, 1000–1700*. New York: W. W. Norton.

Clark G. 1961. *World Prehistory: An Outline*. Cambridge: Cambridge University Press.

Clark G, Huberman M, et al. 1995. A British food puzzle, 1770–1850. *Economic History Review* 2: 215–237.

Cohen A. 1950. Estimating the mean and variances of normal populations from singly truncated and doubly truncated samples. *Annals of Mathematical Statistics* 21: 557–569.

Cole G, Postgate R. [1938] 1976. *The Common People, 1746–1946*. London: Methuen.

Coleman D. 1977. *The Economy of England*. Oxford: Oxford University Press.

Colquhoun P. 1814. *Treatise on the Wealth, Power, and Resources of the British Empire*. London: Joseph Mawmay.

Costa D. 2000. Understanding the twentieth-century decline in chronic conditions among older men. *Demography* 37: 53–72.

Costa D. 2002. Changing chronic disease rates and long-term declines in functional limitation among older men. *Demography* 39: 119–137.

Costa D. 2004. The measure of man and older age mortality: Evidence from the Gould sample. *Journal of Economic History* 64: 1–23.

Crafts N. 1980. Income elasticities of demand and the release of labor by agriculture during the British Industrial Revolution. *Journal of European Economic History* 9: 153–168.

Crafts N. 1985. *British Economic Growth during the Industrial Revolution*. Oxford: Clarendon Press.

Cresswell J, et al. 1997. Is the age of menopause determined in utero? *Early Human Development* 49: 143–148.

Curtin P. 1969. *The Atlantic Slave Trade: A Census*. Madison: University of Wisconsin Press.

Dasgupta P. 1993. *An Inquiry into Well-Being and Destitution*. Oxford: Clarendon Press.

Davenant C. 1699. *An Essay upon the Probable Methods of Making a People Gainers in the Ballance of Trade*. London: James Knapton.

Deane P, Cole WA. 1969. *British Economic Growth, 1688–1959: Trends and Structure*. London: Cambridge University Press.

De Maeyer, E. M. 1976. Protein-energy malnutrition. In *Nutrition and Preventive Medicine*, ed. Beaton G, Bengoa J. Geneva: World Health Organization.

Derry T, Williams T. 1960. *A Short History of Technology*. London: Oxford University Press.

Doblhammer G, Vaupel J. 2001. Life span depends on month of birth. *Proceedings of the National Academy of Sciences of the United States of America* 98: 2934–2939.

Drukker J. 1994. The tradition of anthropometric history in the Netherlands. Presented at National Bureau of Economic Research, Cambridge, MA, July 11–12.

Drukker J, Tassenaar V. 1997. Paradoxes of modernisation and material well-being in the Netherlands during the nineteenth century. In *Health and Welfare during Industrialisation*, ed. Steckel R, Floud R. Chicago: University of Chicago Press.

Drummond J, Wilbraham A. 1958. *The Englishman's Food: A History of Five Centuries of English Diet*. London: Jonathan Cape.

Dyer C. 1983. English diet in the later middle ages. In *Social Relations and Ideas: Essays in Honour of R. H. Hilton*, ed. Aston T, et al. Cambridge: Cambridge University Press.

Elgen I, Sommerfelt K, et al. 2002. Population based, controlled study of behavioural problems and psychiatric disorders in low birthweight children at 11 years of age. *Archives of Child and Fetal and Neonatal Education* 87: F128–F132.

Eveleth PB, Tanner JM. 1976. *Worldwide Variation in Human Growth*. Cambridge: Cambridge University Press.

Everitt A. 1967. The marketing of agricultural produce. In *The Agrarian History of England and Wales: Vol. 4, 1500–1640*, ed. Thirsk J. Cambridge: Cambridge University Press.

Fagan B. 1977. *People of the Earth*. 2nd ed. Boston: Little, Brown.

FAO/WHO/UNU. 1985. *Energy and Protein Requirements: Report of a Joint FAO/WHO/UNU Expert Consultation*. Technical Report Series 724. Geneva: World Health Organization.

Feinstein C. 1988. The rise and fall of the Williamson curve. *Journal of Economic History* 48: 699–729.

Flinn M. 1970. *British Population Growth, 1700–1850*. London: Macmillan.

Flinn M. 1974. The stabilization of mortality in pre-industrial Western Europe. *Journal of European Economic History* 3: 285–318.

Flinn M. 1981. *The European Demographic System, 1500–1820*. Baltimore: Johns Hopkins University Press.

Flinn M. 1982. The population history of England, 1541–1871. *Economic History Review* 35: 443–457.

Floud R. 1984. *The Heights of Europeans since 1750: A New Source for European Economic History*. Working Paper 1318. Washington, DC: National Bureau of Economic Research.

Floud R. 1992. Anthropometric measures of nutritional status in industrialized societies: Europe and North America since 1750. In *Nutrition and Poverty*, ed. Osmani S. Oxford: Clarendon Press.

Floud R, Wachter K, et al. 1990. *Height, Health and History: Nutritional Status in the United Kingdom, 1750–1980*. Cambridge: Cambridge University Press.

Floud R, Fogel R, et al. 2011. *The Changing Body: Health, Nutrition, and Human Development in the Western World since 1700*. Cambridge: Cambridge University Press.

Fogel R. 1986a. Long-Term Changes in Nutrition and the Standard of Living. Presented at Research Topics for Section B7 of the Ninth International Economic History Congress, Berne, Switzerland.

Fogel R. 1986b. Nutrition and decline in mortality since 1700: Some preliminary findings. In *Long-Term Factors in American Economic Growth*, ed. Engerman S, Gallman R. Chicago: University of Chicago Press (for National Bureau of Economic Research).

Fogel R. 1987. Biomedical approaches to the estimation and interpretation of secular trends in equity, morbidity, mortality, and labor productivity in Europe, 1750–1980. Typescript, Center for Population Economics, University of Chicago.

Fogel R. 1989. *Without Consent or Contract*. Vol. 1. New York: W. W. Norton.

Fogel R. 1991. The conquest of high mortality and hunger in Europe and America: Timing and mechanisms. In *Favorites of Fortune: Technology, Growth, and Economic Development since the Industrial Revolution*, ed. Landes D, Higgonet P, Rosovsky H. Cambridge, MA: Harvard University Press.

Fogel R. 1992. Introduction: Notes on the art of empirical research in the social sciences during an age of plunging costs in data processing. In *Without Consent or Contract: Vol. 2. Evidence and Methods*, ed. Fogel R, Galantine R, Manning R. New York: W. W. Norton.

Fogel R. 1993. New sources and new techniques for the study of secular trends in nutritional status, health, mortality, and the process of aging. *Historical Methods* 26: 5–43.

Fogel R. 1994. Economic growth, population theory, and physiology: The bearing of long-term processes on the making of economic policy. *American Economic Review* 84: 369–395.

Fogel R. 1997. Economic and social structure for an aging population. *Philosophical Transactions of the Royal Society of London, Series B* 352: 1905–1917.

Fogel R. 2000. *The Fourth Great Awakening and the Future of Egalitarianism.* Chicago: University of Chicago Press.

Fogel R. 2004a. *Changes in the Process of Aging during the Twentieth Century: Findings and Procedures of the Early Indicators Project.* NBER Working Paper 9941.

Fogel R. 2004b. *The Escape from Hunger and Premature Death: Europe, America, and the Third World, 1700–2100.* New York: Cambridge University Press.

Fogel R, Costa D. 1997. A theory of technophysio evolution, with some implications for forecasting population, health care costs, and pension costs. *Demography* 34: 49–66.

Fogel R, Engerman S. 1974. *Time on the Cross: The Economics of American Negro Slavery.* Boston: Little, Brown.

Fogel R, Floud R. 1991. Nutrition and mortality in France, Britain, and the United States, 1700–1938. Typescript, University of Chicago.

Fogel R, et al. 1978. The economics of mortality in North America, 1650–1910: A description of a research project. *Historical Methods* 11: 75–108.

Fogel R, Engerman S, et al. 1982. *Changes in American and British Stature since the Mid-Eighteenth Century: A Preliminary Report on the Usefulness of Data on Height for the Analysis of Secular Trends in Nutrition, Labor Productivity, and Labor Welfare.* Working Paper 890. Washington, DC: National Bureau of Economic Research.

Fogel R, et al. 1983. Secular changes in American and British stature and nutrition. *Journal of Interdisciplinary History* 14: 445–481.

Fogel R, Lee C, et al. 1986. The aging of Union army men: A longitudinal study. Unpublished manuscript, Cambridge, MA.

Fogel R, Galantine R, et al. 1992. *Without Consent or Contract: The Rise and Fall of American Slavery – Evidence and Methods.* New York: W. W. Norton.

Foreign Office Commission. 1985. *Famine in Africa.* London: Her Majesty's Stationary Office.

Forsén T, et al. 1997. Mother's weight in pregnancy and coronary heart disease in a cohort of Finnish men: Follow-up study. *British Medical Journal* 315: 837–840.

Forste R, Weiss J, et al. 2001. The decision to breastfeed in the United States: Does race matter? *Pediatrics* 108: 291–296.

Frankel S, et al. 1996. Birthweight, body-mass index in middle age, and incident coronary heart disease. *Lancet* 34: 1478–1480.

Fredriks A, et al. 2000. Continuing positive secular growth change in the Netherlands. *Pediatric Research* 47: 316–323.

Freudenberger H, Cummings G. 1976. Health, work, and leisure before the Industrial Revolution. *Explorations in Economic History* 13: 1–12.

Frijhoff W, Julia D. 1979. The diet in boarding schools at the end of the ancién regime. In *Food and Drink in History: Selections from the Annales Economies, Sociétés, Civilisations*, vol. 5, ed. Forster R, Ranum O. Baltimore: Johns Hopkins University Press.

Frisancho A. 1978. Nutritional influences on human growth and maturation. *Yearbook of Physical Anthropology* 21: 174–191.

Frisch R. 1978. Population, food intake, and fertility. *Science* 199: 22–30.

Galenson D. 1982. The Atlantic slave trade and the Barbados market, 1673–1723. *Journal of Economic History* 42: 491–511.

Gopalan C. 1992. Undernutrition: Measurement and implications. In *Nutrition and Poverty*, ed. Osmani S. Oxford: Clarendon Press.

Goubert P. 1960. *Beauvais et the Beauvais de 1600 a 1730.* Paris: Impr. Nationale.

Goubert P. 1973. *The Ancien Régime.* New York: Harper Torchbooks.

Gould B. 1869. *Investigations in the Military and Anthropological Statistics of American Soldiers.* Cambridge: Cambridge University Press.

Graafmans W, et al. 2002. Birth weight and perinatal mortality: A comparison of "optimal" birth weights in seven Western European countries. *Epidemiology* 13: 569–574.

Gras N. 1915. *The Evolution of the English Corn Market from the Twelfth to the Eighteenth Century.* Cambridge, MA: Harvard University Press.

Gray L. 1933. *History of Agriculture in the Southern United States to 1860.* Washington, DC: Carnegie Institution of Washington.

Great Britain. 1833. Report of the factory commissioners of 1883. *Parliamentary Papers* 20.

Grigg D. 1982. *The Dynamics of Agricultural Change: The Historical Experience.* New York: St. Martin's Press.

Hack M, et al. 2002. Outcomes in young adulthood for very-low-birth-weight infants. *New England Journal of Medicine* 346: 149–157.

Hannon J. 1984a. The generosity of antebellum poor relief. *Journal of Economic History* 44: 810–821.

Hannon J. 1984b. Poverty in the antebellum northeast: The view from New York State's poor relief rolls. *Journal of Economic History* 44: 1007–1032.

Hannon J. 1985. Poor relief policy in antebellum New York State: The rise and decline of the poorhouse. *Explorations in Economic History* 22: 233–256.

Harter H, Moore A. 1966. Iterative maximum-likelihood estimation of the parameters of normal populations from singly and doubly censored samples. *Biometrika* 53: 205–213.

Hattersley L. 1999. Trends in life expectancy by social class: An update. *Health Statistics Quarterly* 2: 16–24.

Helleiner K. 1964. The population of Europe from the Black Death to the eve of the vital revolution. In *The Cambridge Economic History of Europe: Vol. 4. The Economy of Expanding Europe in the Sixteenth and Seventeenth Centuries*, ed. Rich E, Wilson C. Cambridge: Cambridge University Press.

Helmchen L. 2003. *Changes in the Pattern of Chronic Disease among Elderly Americans, 1870–2000.* Working paper. Center for Population Economics, University of Chicago.

Himmelfarb G. 1983. *The Idea of Poverty: England in the Early Industrial Age.* New York: Random House.

Holderness B. 1976. *Pre-Industrial England: Economy and Society, 1500–1750.* London: J. M. Dent.

Hollander Z, ed. 1979. *The Complete Handbook of Pro Basketball.* 6th ed. New York: Signet.

Hollingsworth T. 1977. Mortality in the British peerage families since 1600. *Population* 32: 323–352.

Holmes G. 1907. Meat supply and surplus. *U.S. Bureau of Statistics Bulletin* 55: 87–98.

Horton S. 1985. The determinants of nutrient intake: Results from western India. *Journal of Development Economics* 19: 147–162.

Hoskins W. 1964. Harvest fluctuations and English economic history, 1480–1619. *Agricultural History Review* 12: 28–46.

Hoskins W. 1968. Harvest fluctuations and English economic history, 1620–1759. *Agricultural History Review* 16: 15–31.

Hufton O. H. 1974. *The Poor of Eighteenth-Century France.* Oxford: Clarendon Press.

Hufton O. 1983. Social conflict and the grain supply in eighteenth-century France. *Journal of Interdisciplinary History* 14: 303–331.

Jayant K. 1964. Birth weight and some other factors in relation to infant survival: A study on an Indian sample. *Annals of Human Genetics* 27: 261–267.

Jefferis B, Power C, et al. 2002. Birth weight, childhood socio-economic environment, and cognitive development in the 1958 British birth cohort study. *British Medical Journal* 325: 305–308.

Jencks C. 1994. *The Homeless*. Cambridge: Cambridge University Press.

Jordan W. 1959. *Philanthropy in England 1480–1660*. London: Allen and Unwin.

Kanjanapipatkul T. 2001. The effect of month of birth on life span of Union veterans. Typescript, Center for Population Economics, University of Chicago.

Kaplan S. 1976. *Bread, Politics and Political Economy in the Reign of Louis XV*. The Hague: Martinus Nijhoff.

Karpinos B. 1958. Height and weight of Selective Service registrants processed for military service during World War II. *Human Biology* 30: 292–321.

Kemsley W. 1951. Weight and height of a population in 1943. *Annals of Eugenics* 25: 161–183.

Keyfitz N, Flieger W. 1990. *World Population Growth and Aging: Demographic Trends in the Late Twentieth Century*. Chicago: University of Chicago Press.

Kiil V. 1939. *Stature and Growth of Norwegian Men during the Past Two Hundred Years*. Oslo: I Kommisjon hos. J. Dybwad.

King G. 1973. Natural and political observations and conclusions upon the state and condition of England in 1696. In *The Earliest Classics: John Graunt and Gregory King*, ed. Laslett P. Farnborough, Hants: Gregg International.

Komlos J. 1987. Stature, nutrition and economic development in the eighteenth-century Habsburg monarchy: The "Austrian" model of the Industrial Revolution. PhD dissertation, University of Chicago.

Komlos J. 1988. The food budget of English workers: A comment on Shammas. *Journal of Economic History* 48: 149–149.

Komlos J, Cuff T, eds. 1998. *Classics in Anthropometric History*. St. Katharinen, Germany: Scripta Mercaturae.

Koupilová I, Leon D, et al. 1997. Can confounding by sociodemographic and behavioural factors explain the association between size at birth and blood pressure and age 50 in Sweden? *Journal of Epidemiology and Community Health* 51: 14–18.

Kuh D, Power C, et al. 1991. Secular trends in social class and sex differences in adult height. *International Journal of Epidemiology* 20: 1001–1009.

Kumar S. 1987. The nutrition situation and its food policy links. In *Accelerating Food Production in Sub-Saharan Africa*, ed. Mellor J, Delgado C, Blackie M. Baltimore: Johns Hopkins University Press.

Laslett P. 1984. *The World We Have Lost: England before the Industrial Age*. New York: Scribner's.

Lauderdale D, Rathouz P. 1999. Evidence of environmental suppression of familial resemblance: Height among U.S. Civil War brothers. *Annals of Human Biology* 26: 413–426.

Law C, Shiell A. 1996. Is blood pressure inversely related to birth weight? The strength of evidence from a systematic review of the literature. *Journal of Hypertension* 14: 935–941.

Le Brun F. 1971. *Les Hommes et la Mort en Anjou aux 17e et 18e siécles.* Paris: Mouton.

Lee C. 1997. Socioeconomic background, disease, and mortality among Union Army recruits: Implications for economic and demographic history. *Explorations in Economic History* 34: 27–55.

Lee C. 2001. Exposure to disease during growing ages and service. In *Early Indicators of Later Work Levels, Disease, and Death* (program project proposal submitted to the NIA).

Lee R. 1981. Short-term variation: Vital rates, prices and weather. In *The Population History of England, 1541–1871: A Reconstruction*, ed. Wrigley E, Schofield R. Cambridge, MA: Harvard University Press.

Leonard E. 1965. *The Early History of English Poor Relief.* New York: Barnes and Noble.

Lindert P. 1983. English living standards, population growth, and Wrigley-Schofield. *Explorations in Economic History* 20: 131–155.

Lindert P, Williamson J. 1976. Three centuries of American inequality. In *Research in Economic History*, ed. Uselding P. Greenwich, UK: JAI Press.

Lindert P, Williamson J. 1982. Revising England's social tables, 1688–1812. *Explorations in Economic History* 19: 385–408.

Lipson E. 1971. *The Economic History of England: Vols. II and III. The Age of Mercantilism.* London: Adam and Charles Black.

Maddison A. 1991. *Dynamic Forces in Capitalist Development: A Long-Run Comparative View.* Oxford: Oxford University Press.

Maddison A. 2001. *The World Economy: A Millennial Perspective.* Paris: Organisation for Economic Co-operation and Development.

Marshall J. 1968. *The Old Poor Law, 1795–1834.* London: Macmillan.

Martin J, et al. 2002. Births: Final data for 2001. *National Vital Statistics Report* 51: 1–103.

Martorell R. 1985. Child growth retardation: A discussion of its causes and its relationship in health. In *Nutritional Adaptation in Men*, ed. Blaxter KL, Waterlow JC. London: John Libby.

Martorell R, Habicht J-P. 1986. Growth in early childhood in developing countries. In *Methodology: Ecological, Genetic and Nutritional Effects on Growth*, ed. Falkner F, Tanner J. New York: Plenum.

Mata L. 1978. *The Children of Santa María Cauqué: A Prospective Field Study of Health and Growth: A Comprehensive Treatise.* Cambridge, MA: MIT Press.

McCance R, Widdowson E. 1967. *The Composition of Foods.* Report Series 297. London: Medical Research Council Special.

McCormick M, Richardson D. 2002. Premature infants grow up. *New England Journal of Medicine* 346: 197–198.

McMahon M, Bistrian B. 1990. The physiology of nutritional assessment and therapy in protein calorie malnutrition. *Disease-a-Month* 36: 373–417.

McMahon S. 1980. Provisions laid up for the family. Unpublished manuscript.

McNeill W. 1971. *A World History*. 2nd ed. New York: Oxford University Press.

Mellor J, Gavian S. 1987. Famine: Causes, prevention, and relief. *Science* 235: 539–545.

Menken J, Trussell J, et al. 1981. The nutrition fertility link: An evaluation of the evidence. *Journal of Interdisciplinary History* 11: 425–444.

Meuvert J. 1965. Demographic crisis in France from the sixteenth to the eighteenth century. In *Population in History: Essays in Historical Demography*, ed. Glass DV, Eversley DEC. London: Edward Arnold.

Mitchell B, Deane P. 1962. *Abstract of British Historical Statistics*. Cambridge: Cambridge University Press.

Mokyr J. 1985. *Why Ireland Starved: A Quantitative and Analytical History of the Irish Economy, 1800–1850*. London: Allen and Unwin.

Mueller W. 1986. The genetics of size and shape in children and adults. In *Human Growth: Vol. 3. Methodology*, ed. Falkner F, Tanner J. New York: Plenum.

National Bureau of Economic Research. 1980. *Report on the Program of the National Bureau of Economic Research on Long-Term Factors in American Economic Development*. Washington, DC: National Bureau of Economic Research.

O'Brien P, Keyder C. 1978. *Economic Growth in Britain and France 1780–1914: Two Paths to the Twentieth Century*. London: Allen and Unwin.

Osmani S. 1992. On some controversies in the measurement of undernutrition. In *Nutrition and Poverty*, ed. Osmani S. Oxford: Clarendon Press.

Payne P. 1992. Assessing undernutrition: The need for a reconceptualization. In *Nutrition and Poverty*, ed. Osmani S. Oxford: Clarendon Press.

Phelps Brown EH, Hopkins S. 1956. Seven centuries of the price of consumables, compared with builders' wage-rates. *Econometrica* 23: 296–314.

Piggott S. 1965. *Ancient Europe from the Beginnings of Agriculture to Classical Antiquity*. Chicago: Aldine.

Poirier D. 1978. The use of the Box-Cox transformation in limited dependent variable models. *Journal of the American Statistical Association* 63: 284–287.

Population Reference Bureau. 2003. *2003 World Population Data Sheet of the Population Reference Bureau: Demographic Data and Estimates for the Countries and Revions of the World*. Washington, DC: Population Reference Bureau.

Post J. 1976. Famine, mortality, and epidemic disease in the process of modernization. *Economic History Review* 29: 14–37.

Post J. 1977. *The Last Great Subsistence Crisis in the Western World*. Baltimore: Johns Hopkins University Press.

Preston SH, Keyfitz N, Schoen R. 1972. *Causes of Death: Life Tables for National Populations*. New York: Seminar Press.

Pullar P. 1970. *Consuming Passions: Being an Historic Inquiry into Certain English Appetites*. Boston: Little, Brown.

Riley J. 1990a. Long-term morbidity and mortality trends: Inverse health transitions. In *What We Know about Health Transition: The Cultural, Social and Behavioural Determinants of Health: Proceedings of an International Workshop, Canberra, May 1989*. Canberra: Health Transition Centre, Australian National University.

Riley J. 1990b. The risk of being sick: Morbidity trends in four countries. *Population Development Review* 16: 403–432.

Riley J. 1991. The prevalence of chronic diseases during mortality increase: Hungary in the 1980s. *Population Studies* 45: 489–496.

Rona R, Swan A, et al. 1978. Social factors and height of primary schoolchildren in England and Wales. *Journal of Epidemiology and Community Health* 32: 147–154.

Rose M. 1971. *The Relief of Poverty, 1834–1914: Studies in Economic History*. London: Macmillan.

Rose R. 1961. Eighteenth century price riots and public policy in England. *International Review of Social History* 6: 277–292.

Roseboom T, et al. 2000. Coronary heart disease after prenatal exposure to the Dutch famine, 1944–45. *Heart* 84: 596–598.

Rosenzweig M, Schultz T. 1988. The stability of household production technology: A replication. *Journal of Human Resources* 23: 535–549.

Sandberg L, Steckel R. 1987. Heights and economic history: The Swedish case. *Annals of Human Biology* 14: 101–110.

Schmidt I, Jorgensen M, et al. 1995. Height of conscripts in Europe: Is postneonatal mortality a predictor? *Annals of Human Biology* 22: 57–67.

Schofield R. 1983. The impact of scarcity and plenty on population change in England, 1541–1871. *Journal of Interdisciplinary History* 14: 265–291.

Schultz Theodore W. 1980. Prize Lecture. Nobelprize.org. 17 Apr 2012, Available at http://www.nobelprize.org/nobel_prizes/economics/laureates/1979/schultz-lecture.html

Scrimshaw N. 1987. The phenomenon of famine. Mimeograph, Massachusetts Institute of Technology.

Scrimshaw N. 1997. More evidence that foetal nutrition contributes to chronic disease in later life. *British Medical Journal* 315: 825–826.

Scrimshaw N, Gordon J, eds. 1968. *Malnutrition, Learning and Behavior*. Cambridge, MA: MIT Press.

Sen A. 1981. *Poverty and Famines: An Essay on Entitlement and Deprivation*. Oxford: Clarendon Press.

Shammas C. 1983. Food expenditures and economic well-being in early modern England. *Journal of Economic History* 43: 89–100.

Shammas C. 1984. The eighteenth-century English diet and economic change. *Explorations in Economic History* 21: 254–269.

Shammas C. 1988. The food budget of English workers: A reply to Komlos. *Journal of Economic History* 48: 673–676.

Slicher Van Bath BH. 1963. *The Agrarian History of Western Europe, A.D. 500–1850*. London: Edward Arnold.

Sokoloff K, Villaflor G. 1982. The early achievement of modern stature in America. *Social Science History* 6: 453–481.

Soltow L. 1968. Long-run changes in British income equality. *Economic History Review* 21: 17–29.

Srinivasan T. 1992. Undernutrition: Concepts, measurements, and policy implications. In *Nutrition and Poverty*, ed. Osmani S. Oxford: Clarendon Press.

Steckel R. 1979. Slave mortality: Analysis of evidence from plantation records. *Social Science History* 3: 86–114.

Steckel R. 1983. Height and per capita income. *Historical Methods* 16: 1–7.

Steckel R. 1995. Stature and the standard of living. *Journal of Economic Literature* 33: 1904–1940.

Stein C, et al. 1996. Fetal growth and coronary heart disease in south India. *Lancet* 348: 1269–1273.

Stigler G. 1954. The early history of empirical studies of consumer behavior. *Journal of Political Economy* 62: 95–113.

Supple B. 1964. *Commercial Crisis and Change in England, 1600–1642*. Cambridge: Cambridge University Press.

Tanner J. 1959. Boas' contributions to knowledge of human growth and form. *Memoirs of the American Anthropological Association* 89: 76–111.

Tanner J. 1981. *A History of the Study of Human Growth*. Cambridge: Cambridge University Press.

Tanner J. 1982. The potential of auxological data for monitoring economic and social well-being. *Social Scientific History* 6: 571–581.

Tanner J. 1990. *Foetus into Man: Physical Growth from Conception to Maturity*. Cambridge: Cambridge University Press.

Tanner JM. 1993. Review of "Fetal and Infant Origins of Adult Disease," ed. DJP Barker. *Annals of Human Biology* 20: 508–509.

Tanner J, Whitehouse R, et al. 1966. Standards from birth to maturity for height, weight, height velocity, and weight velocity: British children, 1965. *Archives of Disease in Childhood* 41: 454–471.

Teranishi H, Nakagawa H, et al. 2001. Social class differences in catch up growth in a national British cohort. *Archives of Disease in Childhood* 84: 218–221.

Thirsk J. 1983. The horticultural revolution: A cautionary note on prices. *Journal of Interdisciplinary History* 14: 299–302.

Thirsk J. 1985. Agricultural policy: Public debate and legislation. In *The Agrarian History of England and Wales*, vol. VII, ed. Thirsk J. Cambridge: Cambridge University Press.

Tilly C. 1975. Food supply and public order in modern Europe. In *The Formation of National States in Western Europe*, ed. Tilly C. Princeton, NJ: Princeton University Press.

Tilly C. 1983. Food entitlement, famine, and conflict. *Journal of Interdisciplinary History* 14: 333–349.

Tilly L. 1971. The food riot as a form of political conflict in France. *Journal of Interdisciplinary History* 2: 23–57.

Timmer C, Falcon W, et al. 1983. *Food Policy Analysis.* Baltimore: Johns Hopkins University Press.

Toutain J. 1971. La consummation alimentaire en France de 1789 à 1964. *Economies et Sociétés, Cahiers de l'I.S.E.A* 5: 1909–2049.

Trewartha G. 1969. *A Geography of Populations: World Patterns.* New York: John Wiley.

Trussell J, Steckel R. 1978. The age of slaves at menarche and their first birth. *Journal of Interdisciplinary History* 3: 477–505.

Trussell J, Wachter K. 1984. *Estimating Covariates of Height in Truncated Samples.* Working Paper 1455. Washington, DC: National Bureau of Economic Research.

Tucker RS. 1975. Real wages of artisans in London, 1729–1935. In *The Standard of Living in the Industrial Revolution,* ed. Taylor AJ. London: Methuen.

U.S. Bureau of the Census. 1975. *Historical Statistics of the United States, Colonial Times to 1970.* Washington, DC: U.S. Government Printing Office.

U.S. Bureau of Labor. 1903. *Eighteenth Annual Report of the Commissioner of Labor.* Washington, DC: U.S. Bureau of Labor.

U.S. National Center for Health Statistics. 1965. *Weight, Height, and Selected Body Dimensions of Adults: United States 1960–1962.* Washington, DC: U.S. Government Printing Office.

U.S. National Office of Vital Statistics. 1954. Weight and birth and its effect on survival of the newborn in the United States, early 1950. *Vital Statistics Special Report* 39(1).

U.S. Provost-Marshal-General. 1866. Final report 1863–1866. *U.S. House of Representatives Executive Document No. I, 39th Congress 1st Sess.* Series Nos. 1251, 1252, I: 2–163.

Van Wieringen J. 1978. Secular growth changes. In *Human Growth: Vol. 3. Methodology,* ed. Falkner F, Tanner J. New York: Plenum.

Van Wieringen J. 1986. Secular growth changes. In *Human Growth: A Comprehensive Treatise,* ed. Falkner F, Tanner J. New York: Plenum.

Vinovskis M. 1972. Mortality rates and trends in Massachusetts before 1860. *Journal of Economic History* 32: 184–214.

Von Tunzelmann GN. 1979. Trends in real wages, 1750–1850, revisited. *Economic History Review* 32: 33–49.

Waaler HT. 1984. Height, weight, and mortality: The Norwegian experience. *Acta Medica Scandinavica* 679 (Suppl.): 1–51.

Wachter K. 1981. Graphical estimation of military heights. *Historical Methods* 14: 31–42.

Wachter K, Trussell J. 1982. Estimating historical heights. *Journal of the American Statistical Association* 77: 279–303.

Weir D. 1984. Life under pressure: France and England, 1670–1870. *Journal of Economic History* 44: 27–47.

Wilcox A, et al. 1995. Birth weight and perinatal mortality: A comparison of the United States and Norway. *Journal of the American Medical Association* 273: 709–711.

Williamson J. 1985. *Did British Capitalism Breed Inequality?* Boston: Allen and Unwin.

Wilson C. 1973. *Food and Drink in Britain: From the Stone Age to Recent Times*. London: Constable.

Wolfe B, Haveman R. 1990. Trends in the prevalence of work disability from 1962 to 1984, and their correlates. *Milbank Quarterly* 68: 53–80.

World Bank. 1984. *World Development Report 1984*. Washington, DC: World Bank.

World Bank. 1987. *World Development Report 1987*. Oxford: Oxford University Press.

World Bank. 2002. *World Development Report 2003: Sustainable Development in a Dynamic World: Transforming Institutions, Growth, and Quality of Life*. New York: Oxford University Press.

Wrigley E. 1969. *Population and History*. London: Weidenfeld and Nicolson.

Wrigley E. 1987. Some reflections on corn yields and prices in pre-industrial economies. In *People, Cities and Wealth: The Transformation of Traditional Society*, ed. Wrigley E. Oxford: Basil Blackwell.

Wrigley E, Schofield R. 1981. *The Population History of England, 1541–1871: A Reconstruction*. Cambridge, MA: Harvard University Press.

Yasuba Y. 1962. *Birth Rates of the White Population in the United States, 1800–1860*. Baltimore: Johns Hopkins University Press.

Yliherva A, et al. 2001. Linguistic and motor abilities of low-birthweight children as assessed by parents and teachers at 8 years of age. *Acta Paediatrica* 90: 1363–1365.

# Index

The letter *f* following a page number denotes a figure; the letter *t* following a page number denotes a table.